→ You already know the wildly popular creator of the YouTube show You Suck at Cooking by his well-manicured hands and mysterious voice, and now you'll know him for this equally well-manicured and mysterious tome. It contains more than 60 recipes for beginner cooks and noobs alike, in addition to hundreds of paragraphs and sentences, as well as photos and drawings, all of which you can easily confirm by flipping through the pages.

If you bring this book home, you'll learn to cook with unintimidating ingredients in dishes like **Broccoli Cheddar Quiche Cupcake Muffin-Type Things, Eddie's Roasted Red Pepper Dip** (while also learning all about Eddie's sad, sad life), **Jalapeño Chicken,** and also other stuff. In addition, there are cooking tips that can be applied not only to the very recipes in this book, but also to recipes outside of this book, and to all other areas of your life (with mixed results).

In the end, you just might suck slightly less at cooking.*

*Results not guaranteed

◁ P9-BZE-275

YOU SUCK
AT
COOKING

**The Absurdly Practical Guide to
Sucking Slightly Less at Making Food**

CLARKSON POTTER/PUBLISHERS
New York

Copyright © 2019 by Wangjanglers Unlimited Ltd.

All rights reserved.
Published in the United States by Clarkson Potter/Publishers, an imprint
of Random House, a division of Penguin Random House LLC, New York.
clarksonpotter.com

CLARKSON POTTER is a trademark and POTTER with colophon is a
registered trademark of Penguin Random House LLC.

Library of Congress Cataloging-in-Publication Data
Names: Clarkson Potter (Firm), editor.
Title: You suck at cooking : the absurdly practical guide to sucking
    slightly less at making food.
Description: First edition. | New York : Clarkson Potter/Publishers, [2019]
    | Includes index.
Identifiers: LCCN 2018061295 | ISBN 9780525576556 (hardcover) |
    ISBN 9780525576563 (ebook)
Subjects: LCSH: Cooking. | LCGFT: Cookbooks.
Classification: LCC TX714 .Y67 2019 | DDC 641.5 — dc23
    LC record available at https://lccn.loc.gov/2018061295

ISBN 978-0-525-57655-6
Ebook ISBN 978-0-525-57656-3

Printed in China

Book and cover design by Francesca Truman
Photographs by Andrew Thomas Lee

10 9 8 7 6 5 4 3 2 1

First Edition

For Devin.

Just kidding.
For Pimblokto.

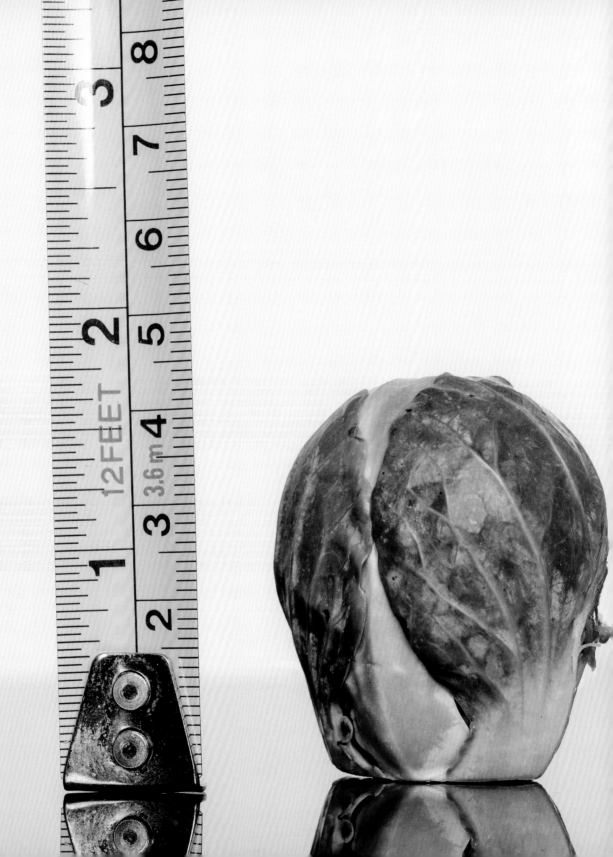

CONTENTS

Introduction   8

Some Basics   13

Breakfast_____48

Dips and Snacks_____70

Sandwiches_____91

Soups and Salads_____116

Veggies on the Side____136

Veggies in the Front____152

Meat, Some Fish,
and Mostly Chicken____168

Desserts_____195

Acknowledgments 216

Index   219

INTRODUCTION

Humans have been eating food for almost as long as they've been alive. Over the past several years, due to the established link between eating food and not dying, food has continued to increase in popularity. I started my You-Tube channel to capitalize on that trend. It was January of 2015 on a cold winter night. Or an unseasonably warm winter morning. Or possibly an overcast afternoon since I'm not an early riser. I had been curious about trying to make tutorial videos for a long time. I was especially curious about whether or not I could make tutorial videos that were entertaining and that were more than just a talking head. So I decided not to include my head. A trickle of people began watching, and over the next couple of years that trickle turned into a stream, then a river, and eventually a frightening hurricane. In a mostly nondestructive way.

Cooking intimidated me well into adulthood. I always thought it would be a great idea to write a cookbook for college students, which I could then go back in time to give to myself. But as I continued to not learn much about cooking (and also struggled with figuring out time travel) I realized I had some mental blocks. I was often too intimidated to try making new things simply because I hadn't tried to

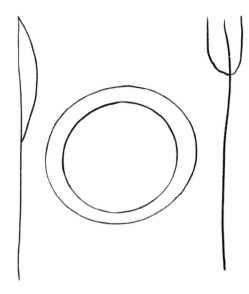

do so before. I wrote this book to be very accessible to people who are new to cooking, who might feel a little intimidated, just like I was. In other words, cowards. They say it takes one to know one. And while that's not true at all, here we are.

I learned what I know of cooking from other tutorial videos, books, recipes, and things I gleaned from my mom and my friends, who totally exist. So if anything in this book is wrong, let me know and I'll pass that along to whoever is actually responsible. Because it's not me. What I hope you get out of this book is that cooking doesn't have to be precious or difficult. All you have to do is follow the instructions and then disobey the instructions whenever you feel like it. Most of the time things will turn out great. And if not great, then at least mostly edible. There's really nothing to be afraid of. I mean, aside from all the terrifying things in the kitchen.

There are sharp things, hot things, lethal machines, and sometimes intruders. You have to know how to handle yourself so you don't get injured and so nobody steals your stuff. And that's on top of the worry that comes with being judged for how that casserole will turn out. This book helps you with that particular situation by not teaching you how to make a casserole.

What this book does contain is simple recipes with a special blend of ridicule and condescension lovingly crafted to spur you on. At the same time, it should be interesting enough to those who aren't intimidated by cooking, who appreciate simple recipe ideas wrapped in Pulitzer-caliber prose. It's for lovers of food and enemies of trees. And it's for anyone who might enjoy a cookbook that attempts not to bore you, but if you do end up bored, or even disappointed, it is thoroughly flammable.

When I make a recipe, I'm looking for the intersection of simplicity and tastiness that is formulated from a mathematical algorithm too complicated for you to understand but that's mostly based on subtraction. I still get intimidated when I see a long ingredient list. And if not intimidated, it makes me want to take a nap. That's why most of the recipes in this book don't have too many ingredients and it's also why there is some ingredient repetition. If you learn how to do a few things well, it can help form a basis for you to try things on your own. It's also just a reflection of my own limitations, which I am pretending is intentional. But my limitations happen to have excellent taste.

Use this book however you want. If you're new to cooking and want to learn some basics, start at the beginning. When you're bored of that, jump to a recipe. If you don't want to cook at all but enjoy absurd humor, read it like a novel. If you enjoy the story I've woven throughout it, you're projecting, because I didn't weave a story throughout it. It's a cookbook, after all. Also, he dies at the end.

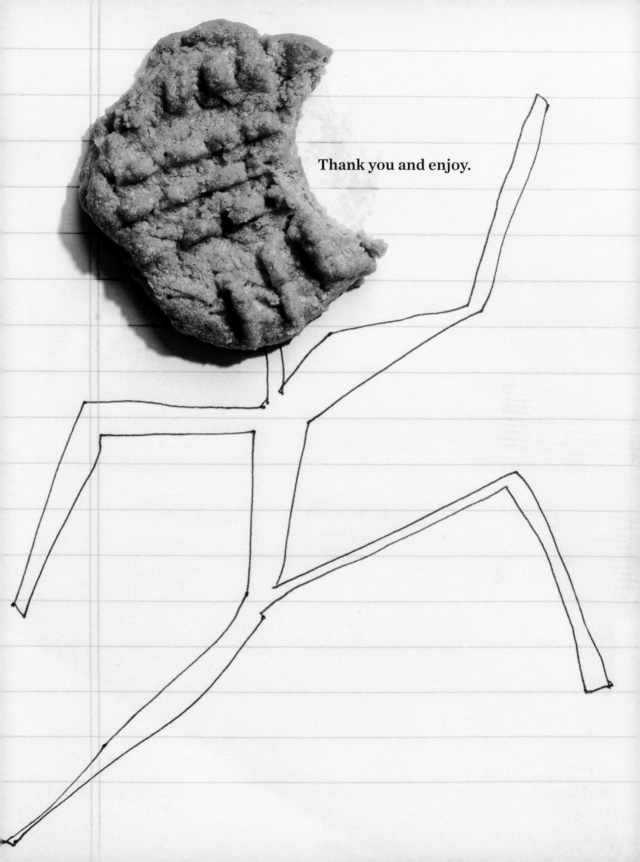

Thank you and enjoy.

SOME BASICS

Volumes could be written about the basics of cooking. Bibles even. Maybe even an entire book or possibly a whole chapter, such as this one. This chapter isn't meant to be comprehensive, just comprehensible. I will not attempt to cover all of the basics, but I will mention a few things that will set you up to cook most of the stuff in this book.

In addition, this information will also set you up to make three to four hundred thousand recipes not in this book. Those recipes can be found in other books, on the Internet, from friends and relatives, from enemies and strangers, scrawled on old withering parchment in thrift stores, dreamed up inside your own mind, or whispered in your ear by dead people. Recipes that come from any other source are not to be trusted and should be immediately discarded.

If you're brand new to cooking, this is the part of the book where I overwhelm you with information to the point of frustration and you don't bother trying. If you are prone to that kind of response, the best way to approach this section is to skip it entirely and go straight to the recipes and try them out. If you insist on reading this chapter, just know that there isn't anything in here that's crucial, except for all of the stuff that is essential, not to mention the few bits that are vital. What I'm saying is, don't feel like you have to go out and buy all of the stuff mentioned in this chapter before you start. There are workarounds for almost anything and I believe in you. Or I am at least willing to say that I believe in you even though I know nothing about you.

THINGS YOU MIGHT NEED

TASTE BUDS

Everything that has ever been cooked has been made to taste. *Someone's* taste. In other words, a recipe is just, like, someone's opinion, man. Try out the recipes as written and adjust parts of them at your leisure. If leisure isn't your thing, adjust things according to your uptight intensity.

Don't like an ingredient? Swap something else in, or don't swap anything in at all. Maybe it will still be good, maybe not. There's one way to find out. And that way is to convince a friend to make it for you, and then try it and see what you think.

The way you can tell if something you made is good is by tasting it. If you like how it tastes, then it is good. If you don't like how it tastes, then it is not good. At least not right now, although it might be good one day, or it might be good right now for someone else. I used to hate onions, but now I can't live without them. That's not an exaggeration. I am hooked up to an onion juice IV in order to keep me alive, because without onions in my blood I have no will to live. High-end chefs might make scrambled eggs that have the texture of hot custard. But if I want to eat something with the texture of hot custard, I'll eat hot custard. And maybe that hot custard will be made of eggs cooked by a high-end chef. Maybe not. The point is, trust your taste, but be open to it evolving. Or don't.

A HEAT SOURCE

Cooking, by definition, involves one or both of two things: combining ingredients and heating them. There are many heat sources to choose from, each more dangerous than the next. Excessive heat can cause pain to any part of the body that contains skin, bones, or living cells. Make sure you choose the heat source that is just dangerous enough for you. Consider the following choices.

FIRE

Using this yellowish, orangish, pointyish, shapeshifting, gas-like substance to cook is a tradition that goes back dozens of years. You really have to keep your wits about you when working with this unpredictable stuff, as many variables affect how it behaves—particularly how angry you're feeling. Also, fire is contagious, so be careful when you get close to it. Luckily, fire usually burns upward as heat normally rises, so you can mostly count on that. I recommend using fire contained in a hard metal box, such as a barbecue. If a barbecue is not available, try cooking over a wild prairie fire.

THE SUN

Cooking with the sun is the trickiest approach, on account of the surface of the sun being almost 10,000°F. This method requires you to expose the food to the sun for no longer than a few millionths of a second, either with quick hand movements or with an astronomically fast rotating rotisserie (best operated by the gusting winds of a Category 5 hurricane). If you cook with the center of the sun, the temperature is closer to 27,000°F, which requires a slightly shorter cooking time, and a very good pair of gloves. Forearm guards are also recommended.

The Kitchen Hot Box is the box inside your kitchen that gets hot. It does so by rapidly removing all of the coldness until there is nothing left but heat. When operating a Kitchen Hot Box, you can choose to make the top hot, the inside hot, or both hot at the same time.

STOVE

A stove is the top part of the Kitchen Hot Box that has burners, which provide you with a controlled source of heat. This can be in the form of flames (see above: Fire), magnetic induction, or electrons moving through metal coils. The stove gives you a safe place to control heat easily while meticulously applying it to food. Many consider using a stove to be cheating, since you don't have to work too hard to make the heat appear. But keep in mind that cheating is the quickest way to get ahead in life so it's probably worth it.

MICROWAVE

The microwave is a neutral-temperature box that heats up the food you put inside it. It does so by hurling very tiny sunbeams at the food, which cause the water molecules inside it to exercise involuntarily until the food is hot.

OVEN

The oven—also known as The Onion, also known as The Undo (pronounced un-doe), also known as the Sizzle Cube, also known as the Danger Cave, also known as the Chamber of Blazing Secrets—is the box part of the Kitchen Hot Box that has a door. If your cooking has so far been limited to the stove and the microwave, get excited to learn how to use one of the most versatile and universal of heat sources. If you already have extensive experience using The Undo, then get excited to continue taking it for granted, even though it continues to be low-key awesome despite your indifference.

Befriend the oven. Sit down with it and tell it your deepest, darkest secrets. That way you'll know you can trust it. If you listen closely, the oven will tell you its deepest, darkest secrets, too. It may sound like nothing because ovens have no secrets.

Whether you're a beginner who has never turned an oven on, mechanically or otherwise, or an experienced chef who has put many things inside the oven, becoming closer to it has many benefits. Primarily, the feeling of closeness.

SOMETHING TO CUT WITH

Choosing a cutting tool is a very personal decision. Before the 1940s when knives were invented, people would simply smash ingredients against the wall. Today, walls are not strong enough to survive being pummeled by onions, let alone potatoes and cabbage. Many houses have been lost to cooks from earlier generations who refused to change their ways. Fortunately, we now have a number of tools at our disposal to dismantle our food:

LASERS

Lasers are a powerful cutting tool. Their application within various industries is widely known and they are highly effective for cutting through most materials, including other lasers. When using a laser to cut food, it is important to have a bunch of disposable countertops on hand, unless your countertop is a mirror, in which case you'll need a disposable kitchen.

TORNADOES

These swirling funnels are composed of fast-moving air, also known as "wind." When wind gets moving in a circle, it can be fast enough to send playing cards through the air at such a high velocity they can cut through trees, which is also fast enough to cut through most fruit and some vegetables. The downside to using a tornado to cut your food is that you are at the mercy of local and international weather systems, and you also risk spilling your food. Effectively using tornadoes in the kitchen requires years of study in order to predict and track tornadoes, as well as a kitchen with a retractable roof.

KNIVES

Knives are most often used to modify the size of objects, particularly if you want to make an object smaller. To cut an object bigger requires elite skill and the ability to move time backward. Until self-chopping vegetables become a thing, we are basically stuck with knives. Attempts to engineer self-chopping vegetables have largely failed. The main approach has been to weave knife DNA into vegetables, which has been consistently rejected by the vegetable DNA because of its preference to survive.

There are two major types of knives: handled knives and handleless knives. I recommend handled knives, as handleless knives often result in too-much-blood in your food, as well as a sore hand. Handled knives are also more widely available and less expensive.

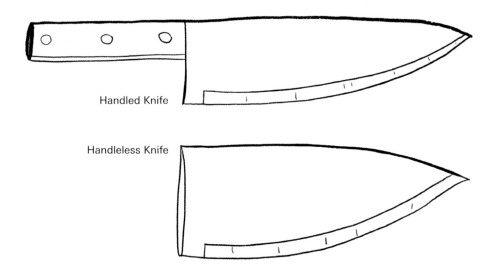

Handled Knife

Handleless Knife

If you're only going to buy one good knife, buy a chef's knife. Also known as a BFK. This is a great knife for chopping onions, other produce, meat, and anything else you put beneath the blade, including other knives. An 8- or 10-inch chef's knife will get most of the jobs done most of the time. A 30-foot-long chef's knife will allow you to dice 16 pounds of vegetables in one chop, but it's very difficult to find a 30-foot-long cutting board, which makes this knife largely useless.

If you're going to buy a second knife, I recommend a paring knife, which is a knife with a flat blade a bit smaller than a steak knife. You can use it to peel things and to get into smaller or trickier places, such as nooks, crannies, crevices, corners, curves, and cracks.

More About Knives

Honing and Sharpening

Using a dull knife sucks. You may not know just how dull your knife is until you use a sharp one. A dull knife is, in some ways, more dangerous as well, as your knife can easily slip off the surface of something you're cutting and lodge itself into something you didn't think you were cutting, such as your common palmar digital artery, which can result in sudden stress on your larynx. So let's keep that knife sharp.

There are two ways to make your knife sharp again: honing and sharpening. Honing is done using a honer. A honer is something that hones. You drag both sides of your blade against it and it straightens out the edge of the blade, making it temporarily sharp again. A honer barely removes any metal, so you can hone a sharpened blade over and over again until the edge is gone. Once the edge is gone, it's time to sharpen, which creates a new edge by removing metal from the blade.

You can take your knives to a professional to get them sharpened, or you can buy a sharpener. Many sharpeners are used by dragging the blade through them, which creates a new edge. You can also get a sharpening stone. This involves imagining how cool it would be to learn the meditative process of sliding your blade against the stone over and over again until it's perfectly sharp, trying it once, then putting it in a drawer where it will sit untouched for six years.

My approach is to use a honer regularly, then take my knives to get sharpened by someone who knows what they're doing every few months. Or much, much longer when my *shawarma* addiction takes over my life, making me realize my knives have been sitting idle, neglected, and covered in dust. Fortunately, a protective coating of dust keeps the blade in tip-top shape.

The Claw Grip

Learning how to use your chef's knife properly is the single most valuable skill you can learn in the kitchen that will make the biggest difference in terms of how quick, easy, and fun it is to cook. When chopping turns from a chore into something you enjoy, cooking becomes a blast. And if not a blast, then at least not-so-difficult and time consuming. And if not not-so-difficult and time consuming, then you need to work harder on your claw grip.

> **Claw Grip Haiku**
>
> **Hand in the claw grip**
> **Slicing up my enemies**
> **Or at least onions**

The Claw Grip helps you keep all human body parts out of the blade's direction of travel.

If you're right-handed, make a claw shape with your left hand, the food-holding hand, so that your fingertips are tucked under, and your second knuckles are sticking out. Use that hand to hold whatever you're chopping—let's say it's a scallion. Hold your knife in your right hand, sharp side down with your thumb and index finger gripping the blade where it meets the handle, and press the side of the blade up against the protruding knuckles of your left hand. Slice the scallion, then work your left claw along the scallion, while keeping the blade pressed against your knuckles. If you are left-handed, do the same thing, but the opposite, or take a picture of this page in a mirror and follow the instructions as written.

By using the Claw Grip, you rely more on *feel*, rather than *vision*, when chopping. You also keep your digits out of the way of the blade 100 percent of the time, which is scientifically known to be the correct amount. This method feels awkward at first, but like most new skills, it starts to feel normal very quickly. Commit to learning the Claw Grip and you will be surprised by how rapidly you improve and how easy chopping becomes.

You also might garner a few compliments from people watching you, such as "Say, you're really good at chopping," or "Impressive, the way you're able to chop that scallion even though your hand is all clumped up in a weird-looking ball," or "It seems you are far better at chopping than you are at being a good friend." Comments such as these will help to set you up for success and will confirm that you made the right decision to learn a new skill to improve your life rather than investing more time in your personal relationships.

WANGJANGLER

A good wangjangler, also known by its more offensive and inappropriate name, "spatula," is a great tool for manipulating food in a hot skillet while not burning your hands (which is both painful and dangerous, also known as paingerous). Another tool that can be used to manipulate food is psychology. But who really understands the mind of a tomato? That's why the wangjangler is the first choice for food manipulation among chefs worldwide.

Metal wangjanglers are good for pans without a nonstick surface, such as cast iron or stainless steel. Plastic or silicone wangjanglers are good for nonstick pans. Wangjanglers with an entirely flat surface, with no grill (see diagram, opposite), are easiest to clean and my favorite for cooking eggs, which tend to stick like glue in the cracks of the grill. Wangjanglers also come in the shape of a large spoon. In fact, anything that is used to flip, mix, wrassle, or stir your food is a wangjangler. Because wangjangling is a state of mind.

Wangjangling Pro Tips

➡ Wangjanglers are magnetic, which is why food sticks to them. Use a fork to scrape the magnetized food back into the pan.

➡ Use the wangjangler to flip hot things.

➡ Do not form your hand into the shape of a wangjangler and attempt to flip hot things while saying, "Look at me, I'm a wangjangler!" with a high falsetto.

OVEN GLOVES

An oven glove is useful when holding things that are very hot, such as pans that have just been inside the oven, or my triceps. You can use a kitchen towel to handle a hot pan, but an oven glove gives you far better protection and is way easier. Unlike the kitchen towel, the oven glove can also be useful when shaking someone's hand, to avoid contamination and intimacy (both of which can ruin a great meal). If you're cooking a lot, consider also getting oven pants.

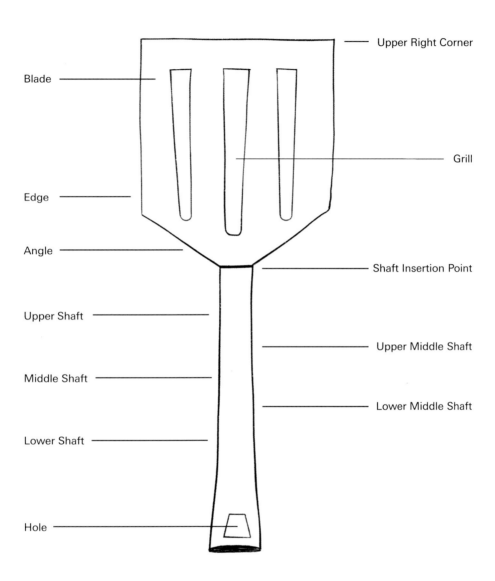

Blade

Upper Right Corner

Grill

Edge

Angle

Shaft Insertion Point

Upper Shaft

Upper Middle Shaft

Middle Shaft

Lower Middle Shaft

Lower Shaft

Hole

SAUCEPAN

The saucepan, also known as a "pot," is a handled, metal, heat-resistant tub that's great for making sauces, soups, anything liquidy, and giving small objects a bath. Its high, protective walls shelter the sauce from the outside world, allowing it to bubble away without sputtering and splattering all over your perfect life. It looks like this:

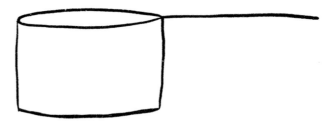

Storing several stacked saucepans on standby for simmering soups, stews, stocks, or sauces is stunningly smart for satisfying your stomach when you are seriously salivating or slightly starving.

THE SKILLET

A skillet is a pan with slanted sides. Like all pans, it keeps the food above the heat, preventing it from falling into the space beneath the burner, which sometimes happens when you cook with no pan at all. It's also easier to clean a skillet rather than putting the entire stove into the sink, which is especially dangerous if you have electric burners.

The reason a skillet is called a skillet is because it takes more skill to keep the food inside it than a pan with nonslanted sides. Those non-slanted pan walls allow you to wrassle with total abandon. The skillet teaches you the physics of responsibility.

The proper way to use a skillet is to hold the handle, then place the flat, round, slanted-edge part onto the burner. The improper way to use the skillet is to hold the flat, round, slanted-edge part and place the handle on the burner. This improper way is also very ineffective, unless you are cooking a single piece of asparagus and are good at balancing.

What kind of skillet should you get? For a beginner, I recommend a nonstick skillet as your go-to stovetop pan, mainly because it's easier to clean. If you have a frustrating time getting gunk off your pan, you might never cook again. But there are many options. The variety of pan choices available is so extensive that it's beyond my ability to summarize, let alone comprehend. So good luck with your research.

BAKING SHEET AND PARCHMENT PAPER

The baking sheet is the simplest and most versatile cooking surface used inside your oven. It looks like this, except it's usually larger:

Parchment paper is a paper that won't burn in the oven (but will burn if you take a lighter to it, trust me) and that keeps you from having to scrub gunk off your baking sheet every time you use it. Actually it will also burn if you have it on the top rack on broil for too long, or if you're baking over an open bonfire. It greatly reduces the amount of water needed to clean the pan. If you are concerned about wasting too much paper, choose a brand of parchment paper that comes from 100% Certified Evil Trees.

A CUTTING BOARD

A cutting board is a board that you cut things on. It keeps your counter clean and scratch-free. Often confused with a baking sheet, it looks like this:

When selecting a cutting board, make sure you don't use one that is too small for what you are chopping, as it ends up making more work for you since you have to use extra dexterity to keep your ingredients from spilling off the board. And we all know how much dexterity you have— not very much. While a small cutting board is easy to wash and can be useful for chopping items with a very small volume, such as scallions or garlic, it can also unconsciously hold you back while chopping larger items, which is mentally exhausting. I recommend an 18 × 12-inch cutting board at minimum, for chopping onions or anything larger. Feel free to build a cutting board arsenal for various purposes.

MIXING BOWLS

Mixing things together when ingredients are nearly spilling over the edge is annoying and slows you down. It's not just a bowl. It's a *vessel of wangjanglitude.* If you're someone who likes to wangjangle with an exceptional amount of passion, forcing your food into a smaller bowl will leave you emotionally stunted. Get some bigger bowls and really go to town. Put your hips into it. Into the mixing, not into the bowl.

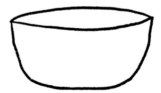

MEASURING CUPS AND SPOONS

Measuring devices are great for wasting time in the kitchen by making you check several drawers to find the proper teaspoon that is perpetually lost. The best approach to this ubiquitous problem is to make a Measuring Cup Bracelet™ and to wear it at all times. This solution has the secondary benefit of making it easy to measure your water usage when you are in the shower, so you can make sure you are wasting the appropriate amount. This solution has the thirdiary benefit of making a constant jangling sound when you're walking around, which keeps you safe from bears, and lets your friends know when you're coming (so they have ample time to hide). It also has the fourthiary benefit of starting a new fashion trend. But beware: Once the fashion trend comes and goes and everyone is throwing their measuring cup bracelets in the garbage, you're going to look like an unfashionable loser. But at least we'll look like unfashionable losers together.

Just kidding. I would never wear a measuring cup bracelet.

INSTANT-READ THERMOMETER

An instant-read thermometer is mostly used to measure the temperature of meat, although it's sometimes used to measure the temperature of inanimate animals. The last two words of that sentence come from one of the sickest bars I've ever dropped during a rap battle, which took place in 2004, in a dark basement club inside the Metro Detroit area of my mind. Yes, it was a taxidermy-based burn.

SOME IMPORTANT INGREDIENTS

SALT

Salt is a mineral that comes from the ground, sea, or air. All salt is chemically identical, composed of the elements sodium and chlorine. However, combining sodium and chlorine is not a suitable salt substitute. The only suitable substitute for salt is salt.

Table salt is ground salt, which is really sea salt that's been in the ground so long it has forgotten where it came from. It is often iodized, meaning iodine, a critical micronutrient, is added to it. This is often seen as the least-good-tasting salt by people who are into salt, and people who are into salt are often the most susceptible to marketing hype.

Kosher salt, which can come from the ground or seawater, usually has bigger, uneven crystals. It is less refined than table salt and is used for all parts of the cooking process, but is especially good for adding salty crunch. Fine kosher salt is similar in crystal size to table salt.

Sea salt comes from the sea. It is very similar to ocean salt, since it is made from the same substance: salt. These two types of salt also spent most of their lives bathing in the same liquid: salt water. Sea salt comes in a variety of crystal sizes, including coarse and fine. Fine sea salt is what I use for the recipes in this book, but table salt and fine kosher salt will give you a similar result.

Air salt is the rarest salt of them all. Much like dark energy, it is so difficult to detect that it has yet to be photographed, let alone tasted.

The main thing to keep in mind when swapping out one salt for another is the difference in the crystal size. One teaspoon table salt or fine sea salt will contain a lot more salt than 1 teaspoon kosher salt or course sea salt due to the larger size of those crystals, so adjust accordingly. Or just do what I did and use fine sea salt. As someone who's really into salt, I can assure you that sea salt definitely tastes the best.

Food can be salted before, during, or after cooking and is often adjusted throughout the cooking process. When using ground salt, be mindful that the salt was already buried for millions of years, so reburying it inside your food may be considered disrespectful.

PEPPER

Also known by its scientific name, *Pepper pepper pepper*, pepper is one of the world's most common spices. Sailors used to have pouches of it tied to their belts because the food they ate didn't taste good without it, much like many foods today, and also because pepper shakers would slide off the table whenever their ships hit a wave. Carrying the pepper this way also created a localized spice barrier, which was effective for repelling mermaids.

Freshly ground pepper tastes much better than preground pepper, objectively speaking. It's one of the simplest ingredient changes you can make to improve the taste of your cooking. But if you're sticking with preground, good for you. Don't let anyone boss you around.

While I am normally a stickler for using the scientific name for ingredients, I will be using the term "pepper" throughout the book as opposed to the more correct *Pepper pepper pepper*. The reason is because of the printer ink cartels. They have been steadily driving up prices for decades, and I refuse to give them more money than necessary. That's also the reason this book sticks to the facts, and only the facts, and writes them in the quickest, tidiest, and most efficient way, whenever it is even remotely possible to do such a thing, but never when it's not possible to do that thing I just mentioned in this very sentence, which you are currently still reading on account of the fact that you are still looking at these words while your brain processes the information and your mind creates meaning out of these shapes and symbols so that you might understand what is being talked about, or written about rather, as there is no talking happening whatsoever

unless you happen to be speaking this out loud in which case you are in an excellent position to appreciate the rhythm and cadence with which this sentence has been meticulously constructed in terms of it not only being straight to the point but also well crafted, at least in your opinion, which is a good one.

COOKING OIL

Extra virgin olive oil is one of the most common cooking oils and is great for most things. But for high temperatures, extra virgin olive oil isn't the best since it has a lower smoke point and will generate free radicals when it gets too hot. That might sound awesome, on account of them being both free and radical, but they're actually not good for you.

Extra-light olive oil, vegetable oil, avocado oil, peanut oil, grapeseed oil, canola oil, sunflower oil, and safflower oil are some of the oils that are better for cooking at high temperatures. Coconut oil is another popular cooking oil that is good for a variety of temperatures, but beware: It tastes faintly of coconut.

Most of the time you'll want to add ingredients to the pan when the oil is hot. One way to tell that the oil is hot is when it moves around the pan like water. Another way to tell is when the oil appears to glisten or shimmer. When the oil is shimmering like the surface of a lake under the light of the full moon on a crisp autumn night, it's time to add the ingredients.

ONIONS

Onions can be found in 99.999% of anything that's ever been cooked. They can also be found in 47% of anything that's never been cooked. You may not see them, but they're there. And even if those numbers aren't exactly correct, I believe I've made my point. My point is that you can't trust my statistics. But what you can trust is that onions make everything taste great as long as you like the taste of onions, and as long as you are not cooking something that does not go well with onions.

Onions come in a variety of flavors and a variety of shapes. Some have more sweetness, some are milder, and some, like the scallion—the green onion—deserve to have a religion founded upon them. For the purposes of this book, don't worry too much about which onion you're using if you can't find the specific one that's called for. Cooking onions are a great all-around onion, and my general favorite spherical onion is the red onion. Sure, it tastes great, but I also just have a weakness for mislabeled colors. Either it's purple or I am color-blind. You be the judge. But also keep your opinion to yourself.

Learning how to properly dice an onion will make you very efficient in the kitchen. Use these steps below, but also see the Claw Grip on pages 20–21.

➜ Cut your onion in half from top to bottom, cutting through the stem and root, but leaving the stem on.

➜ Remove the peel, or if it's particularly sticky, remove the peel and outer layer.

➜ Lay one half, flat side down, on your cutting board, with the stem toward your nonknife palm.

➜ Make slices down the onion, $\frac{1}{2}$ an inch in from the stem, $\frac{1}{4}$ inch apart.

➜ Make $\frac{1}{4}$-inch-wide slices across the onion, and watch as your onion is reduced to perfect mini pieces.

➜ Be careful when you are cutting on the curve closest to your onion-holding hand, because if your knife slips, it will slip toward your hand. Instead, lay the newly cut flat side of the onion down on the cutting board and continue chopping.

➜ Discard the stem.

➜ Use the onion.

GARLIC

Garlic has a flavor profile similar to onions. Chopping garlic can feel like it takes forever because of the size-to-accomplishment ratio. You're pretty much using the same amount of chops for a clove of garlic as you are for an onion, but you're getting much less volume. But the flavor of garlic is so much more powerful that the work-to-results ratio is probably similar on a taste level. But that doesn't make it feel like less of a giant waste of time.

One approach to speed up the time it takes to chop a clove of garlic is to allow yourself to age for twenty to thirty years before making your next attempt. The more you age, the faster time feels like it's moving. What may feel like the longest two minutes of your life now will feel like microseconds in a few decades, and you'll actually enjoy those microseconds in the future. Einstein wrote extensively about this in his theory of relativity, I'm pretty sure.

If chopping garlic feels too annoying, so much so that you're not going to cook something because of it, I suggest using prechopped garlic from a jar, or at least have the option on standby until you learn how to mince garlic hella quick. If you do that, 1 garlic clove is equivalent to about ½ tablespoon chopped or 1 teaspoon minced. You can also get a garlic press, which will smash your garlic up in one squeeze of a lever, reducing your chopping time to 0 seconds. You'll spend the same amount of time cleaning the garlic press as you would have just chopping the garlic, maybe longer, but making easier choices now that end up being difficult later is part of human nature.

When a recipe calls for chopping garlic, or any vegetable, for that matter, here is what I mean:

Roughly Chopped: pieces around ¾ inch

Chopped: pieces around ½ inch

Diced: pieces around ¼ inch

Finely Chopped: pieces around ⅛ inch

Minced: pieces around $\frac{1}{16}$ inch and smeared against the cutting board with your knife to crush them further

Obliterated: pieces chopped so small you are now breathing the garlic

But what if a recipe calls for finely chopped garlic but you don't quite chop the pieces that small? Is this something crucial that you should worry about? Well let me tell you, if you don't chop garlic quite as small as is called for, there's a chance it could end up slightly less cooked than intended. But is the chef who created the recipe going to come to your house and yell at you for not following it exactly? I hope so. That would be hilarious.

BROTH

Broth can be homemade or store-bought in liquid form ready to use, in liquid form ready to be watered down, or in liquidless form, ready to be watered up (bouillon). It's the basis of most soups, but can also be used to cook rice or quinoa or make sauces, or can be consumed on its own. It can be vegetarian, chicken, beef, or some other things I'd rather not talk about.

HOT SAUCE

Hot sauce is dangerous, like a drug. Once you start using, it quickly becomes addictive and food quickly becomes bland without it. It is nearly on par with caffeine in terms of addictions that are totally worth it. If you can't handle the heat, start with a few atoms of hot sauce and work

your way up until you can eat an entire molecule, then keep going until you can eat an entire ghost pepper plant including the leaves, roots, and dirt. That's when you know you're cool with hot sauce.

ADJUSTING FLAVOR

Figuring out how to make something taste better can feel daunting. That's why I have devised a simple system to guide you through the process of adjusting and enhancing flavor on the fly. When cooking, pay attention to these four simple components:

<u>Acid</u>

<u>Salt</u>

<u>Sweetness</u>

<u>Seasoning</u>

Also known as the ASSS system of food flavoring, this approach will often help you answer the question: What's missing? (But only in relation to food. Sorry.) There are many approaches to fine-tuning a dish's flavor, but none have the elegant simplicity of the ASSS system. Let's take a crack at the ASSS approach to see if we can unravel its mysteries.

ACID

Most recipes contain some form of acid. Vinegar, lemon or lime juice, and tomatoes are among the most common sources. The reason foods are often finished with a squeeze of lemon is not just because yellow things taste good. It's because acid, like salt, is a flavor enhancer that brings other flavors together and makes them all taste better. Acid can brighten a dish and often completes it. It's part of the reason tomatoes and pickles go so well in sandwiches. It's why guacamole without lime is just a bowl of green stuff. It's why vinegar is in so many dressings. If you're cooking a dish and you feel like something is missing, consider acid. If you're cooking a dish and your skillet starts levitating before taking you on a multi-dimensional journey where you understand the illusion of time and the beginning of infinity, then you've used the wrong type of acid.

SALT

Here we go again. This stuff is crucial. Salt isn't in literally everything simply because people like the taste of salt; it's in literally everything because salt is made of magical flavor enhancement crystals that not only help food realize its full potential, but also help you realize your full potential because if you don't eat salt, you die. This is why salt is the entry point of the ASSS system and should be at the beginning of this list. But if it was, not only would it create the distracting acronym SASS, it would also result in poorer tasting food since any dish can be ruined by too much attitude.

Learning how to salt your food just right is a skill, and there are several ways to go about it. If you're winging it, start with less salt and keep tasting until the level is just right, like Goldilocks (minus the terrifying risk of being ripped apart by bloodthirsty bears who were just protecting their home from an intruder). Seek the salting saturation sweet spot. Creep up to the edge but do not go over.

When boiling vegetables or pasta, salt the water generously so if you were to take a sip of it, you'd probably gag or at least make a very sour face. With rice and quinoa, ½ teaspoon fine salt per cup of uncooked is a good general rule but trust your own taste. If you're making a soup or stew, a lot of the salt may come from the broth or bouillon, and you'll have to decide if more is needed. Salt is in cheese as well, so finishing a dish with parmesan or crumbled feta may be all that's needed to complete the flavor.

If you're making a big pot of something that needs to be salted and you're not sure how much salt to use, try a technique I call Matrix Visualization™. Estimate in inches the height of the food in your pot. Now add salt as if the entire surface were a plate of scrambled eggs, then do it again until you've hit the number of inches. Then bend backward and dodge a series of bullets while watching life pass by in two thousand frames per second. Then taste and see if it's good, or if you've ruined it with too much salt. If you started with broth, then that was probably too much.

If you go too far, the main solution is adding more unsalted ingredients, although you might be able to balance a slight oversalting with acid or sugar. You may find you have a higher or lower salt tolerance than someone you eat with regularly. Keep this in mind if you're cooking for others, and leave room for the salt to be adjusted individually. Another way to deal with oversalted food that you've made for someone else is to create a distraction whenever they take a bite. Alternatively, break some horribly tragic news that will cause them to start crying. The salt lost in their tears will result in a salt deficiency in their body, which will balance out the taste in their mouth.

SWEETNESS

Sweetness is another important balancing factor when building a satisfying flavor. A touch of honey balances out the vinegar (i.e., acid) in many salad dressings. Acids are sour and sweetness is the antidote. If a dish is too acidic, it can be balanced with a bit of sugar, such as when making a tomato sauce. Sometimes that sugar comes from caramelizing the onions, and often that is enough. (To be clear, onions become sweet when caramelized [to be clearer, caramelizing onions means cooking them slowly until they turn brown and taste much sweeter.])

In many recipes, one type of sugar can be swapped for another. If you don't have maple syrup, you might try honey or brown sugar instead. While you may miss the maple flavor, when the sweetness level is adjusted correctly, your dish overall should still taste good. If you have light brown sugar instead of dark, or vice versa, the change will rarely be noticeable unless you are a trained molasses expert. If you swap in brown sugar for white, make sure the brown sugar is packed into the measuring cup to match the density of the white sugar.

Don't keep yourself from cooking something just because you don't have the specific type of sugar on hand. Surely there are many examples where the type of sugar is crucial, but I'm feeling too lazy to look them up right now.

SEASONING

While salt is the most important aspect of flavoring, seasoning is by far the deepest component of the ASSS system. Paradoxically, seasoning can also include salt, acid, and sugar. Figure that one out why don't you.

Seasoning is the specific flavoring you add to your ingredients. It can include herbs, spices, garlic, or anything else that tastes like anything. If you add something that tastes like nothing, then it is not seasoning.

When seasoning, you have two choices: (1) follow the recipe or (2) freestyle. By freestyle, I mean start simple and add things you think might work. If you're not sure whether or not a flavor will work with what you're making, take a small portion or spoonful of the dish and add a very tiny amount of the herb, spice, or sauce, then taste. You'll know right away. You can also use this method to figure out if you need more salt.

I wish I had done that the time I decided to add dill to guacamole. That was not good. That was years ago. I still haven't let it go. I had just discovered the magic of dill, arguably the greatest herb of all time, and I was sure that dill was great in everything. It is not great in everything. It was not great in that guacamole. It was a big mistake. I'll get over it, someday. You don't have to worry about me. Just keep in mind that cooking based on color alone doesn't always work.

In conclusion, by always eating ASSS system–based food, you will ensure that the flavors of your dish turn out well. By diving into every component of the ASSS system and exploring it deeply, you will set yourself up to create dishes that are full-flavored, and you will learn to hone the taste of your meals, I hope.

REMEMBER FAT

We don't use oil and butter to cook simply because it keeps food from sticking to the skillet. We also use it because it affects the flavor, texture, and overall balance of any dish. Know that fat is not evil and it is often a crucial part of how something tastes. Think mayo or cheese on a sandwich, oil in a stir-fry, butter with fried eggs, butter on toast, butter on noodles, butter in muffins, butter literally caked over my entire body because I heard it was good for me in a magazine that one time or at least that's what I tell my friends, but really I just love covering myself in butter. There's no place for judgment in cooking.

Except when it comes to air fryers. Not only do air fryers remove fat from the cooking process (which is part of what makes food taste great), but they also fry up one of the most crucial substances for both living creatures and birds alike: air. Without air, living creatures have nothing to breathe, and birds have nothing to fly in. We can only hope that the dangerous trend of frying air fizzles out (and is hopefully replaced by water frying) before air becomes too expensive for everyone.

BURN THINGS

How many times have you heard someone exclaim, with shock and sadness, "Oh no, the carrots are browning!" Hopefully never, because when food starts to brown it tastes way more awesome than it did before. Most of the time. It's not exactly burning, mind you. That was click bait. Or in this case, paragraph bait.

When food browns, it's called the Maillard reaction, because Mr. Maillard was the first person to articulate it, a long time ago, and he explained that something happens with the proteins in the food when it's heated a certain amount and it ends up tasting good as a result. Think toast, toasted marshmallows, seared steak, caramelized onions, and baked cookies. Also other things. Don't be afraid to brown the things that will taste better that way. Don't brown the things that won't. Also be mindful not to burn things, which is known as the Maillard overreaction.

Similar to the Maillard reaction, the Uncle Jerry reaction is another cooking-related process. It's the quickly building tension that ruins a backyard picnic when someone wanders over after a few cocktails and tries to tell Uncle Jerry how to use his own barbecue.

THE MENTAL GAME

Overcoming mental obstacles is the most difficult part of cooking for many people. You might not want to try cooking because you'll be embarrassed about making something that doesn't turn out well. You also might not want to try cooking because you could find out that you're really good at it, and then you'll have to spend the rest of your life wrestling with your own greatness. But it's more likely that you're just lazy. The good news is that as you do it more, it gets exponentially easier. And while I can't verify the accuracy of the exponentiality of the progression, I can testify to the likelihood of it not mattering that I mentioned it in the first place. Let's address your blocks:

MENTAL BLOCK #1: It Might Suck

Here's how recipes work: You read the recipe, you follow the instructions, and everything turns out well almost all of the time. There is so much leeway in most recipes in relation to the ingredient amounts and the cooking times that it is truly difficult to mess a recipe up beyond the point of no return. In fact, if you do mess it up past the point of no return, it's almost more impressive than if it turns out well. Having said that, you *will* make something that sucks at some point. The trick is to laugh at yourself. Laugh and laugh and laugh, and then laugh some more until it is so uncomfortable that the people you are serving the food to are way more concerned about your well-being than they are about how poor the food tastes.

MENTAL BLOCK #2: Using New Equipment

I realized I had a mental block around using the oven when a friend asked me to make a yam recipe while she was at work all day. I was staying at her place, so it felt rude to say no. It felt that way because it would have been rude to say no. I immediately started making excuses in my head, but it all boiled down to one simple thought: I didn't know how. But "I didn't know how" simply meant "I haven't tried." I didn't realize at the time that an oven was nothing more than a giant toaster flipped on its side with a large steel door, and so I stared into the abyss of the unknown.

If you've never cooked something you've wanted to cook because you don't know how to use an oven, hand mixer, immersion blender, or anything else: JUST STOP IT. And by that, I mean, JUST START IT. Start using those things. Make mistakes. Have fun. Be less cowardly. If you've ever operated a common jackhammer, using any of these tools will be a breeze.

MENTAL BLOCK #3: Cooking for Someone Else

Cooking for someone else can be terrifying. It can cause your hypothalamus to jack up your adrenal-cortical and sympathetic nervous systems until you don't know whether or not you should sprint out of the kitchen at maximum speed or attack a saucepan with no mercy.

While it may seem daunting, something is working in your favor when you cook for someone else. People are more forgiving of food that you make for them than they are of food they make for themselves, because you are making them food, and making someone food is an awesome thing to do. If they don't love it, they should at least pretend it's pretty good. But most important, even if they don't love it, and even if they don't pretend it's pretty good, they should be grateful AF that you made it for them. And if you've spent a good part of your life with someone making food for you, then it might be time to return the favor.

If you're concerned that what you're making doesn't taste very good, one way to balance this out is to act very obnoxious. This will make the food taste far better than your personality feels, and they will leave thinking "Man, that person really knows how to cook. I can't wait to never see him again." If they live in the same house as you, this strategy might need a rethink.

MENTAL BLOCK #4: The Speed of Time

Sometimes the effort we put into cooking feels like a huge waste of time. You may find yourself asking the question "Why should I cook when I can be doing something else?" The best answer to this question is to cook *while* doing something else. My mom likes to watch movies while she cooks. I like listening to podcasts or new music. Old music, too. Any age music, really. That stuff sounds good no matter how long it's been around. Sometimes musical notes need time to mature before you really get that full sound. Especially with the bassoon.

If you're truly desperate, you can attempt cooking while practicing the art of conversation with another human being, which can also help speed up time. However, in this situation you run the risk of developing bonds that could lead to memorable experiences and emotions. Tread carefully.

As an absolute last resort, you can attempt to enjoy cooking all alone, while practicing something called "mindfulness." It's a frightening form of self-manipulation where you just focus on what you're doing without thought, which results in the feeling that you're enjoying it without the need to distract yourself with anything else at all. Here, the danger of becoming enlightened is all too real, for if you learn to enjoy this activity by yourself, there's a real threat of transcending time and experiencing a deep sense of peace and harmony with the world around you. This is a real hassle because it will inevitably lead to you having to replace all of your friends.

MENTAL BLOCK #5: Cleaning

Cleaning sounds like a physical obstacle, but don't be fooled. Time slows down exponentially when cleaning if you don't want to be cleaning. The trick is to make yourself want to clean. Multitasking once again comes into play with music, audiobooks, podcasts, or conversation, but there's another element to timing here.

Much of the cleaning you need to do can be done while you're cooking. You may feel resistant to tarnishing the cooking process with object-bathing, but if you make a point of cleaning anything you're done with as you go, you'll be surprised at how little is left over at the end. Pots, pans, and wangjanglers that are still warm from cooking are far easier to clean than when they cool down and the food hardens into cement, but be careful not to burn yourself.

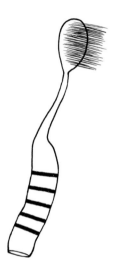

Finally, consider a few tools to help you overcome this block. My most-used cleaning implement is a plastic scrub brush. I've had the same one for years. It rinses off cleanly and can be thrown in the dishwasher. When using this brush, you're not washing a dish with a microscopic version of everything else a sponge or dishcloth has ever come into contact with. The scrub brush does not invoke the natural repulsion you might feel when reaching for a wet, disgusting rag. If you are going to use a rag, replace it daily, because it's a bacteria-growing Petri cloth.

The other main tool I suggest is a pair of rubber gloves. They keep a layer between your skin and the disgustitude, they allow you to use hotter water than you can without them, and they generally remove any residue-based reluctance you might have to getting your hands in there.

While cleaning is a mental block, it is also the most important physical block to preparing food. No one wants to cook in a dirty kitchen. Make yourself a promise and make a pact with everyone you live with: We will always leave the kitchen clean.

The key to always leaving the kitchen clean is to never leave the first cup. Don't ever, ever, ever give anyone else a reason to leave the second cup, not even your future self. Because now you have an excuse to leave the third cup, and then you're playing a very dangerous game indeed. The game is called Dirty Kitchen and everyone's a loser.

Now let's say it together, out loud. WE WILL ALWAYS LEAVE THE KITCHEN CLEAN. Okay, one more time, louder. WE WILL ALWAYS LEAVE THE KITCHEN CLEAN. Now tattoo it on your face. WE WILL ALWAYS LEAVE THE KITCHEN CLEAN. Come back and continue reading once the swelling has reduced and the regret has calmed.

HOW TO COOK ALMOST ANYTHING

Let's take a quick look at an easy way to cook most things that allows you to enjoy the natural flavor of the food. While there are instructions for every recipe in this book, you can use these methods to take your newfound knowledge outside the confines of these pages. But always, always, credit me regardless.

COOK ANYTHING METHOD #1: Roasting

Preheat your oven to 350° or 400°F. Line a baking sheet with parchment paper and put the thing you want to cook on it. Drizzle on some olive oil, then sprinkle on some salt and pepper.

Put it in the oven for 10 to 20 minutes, then check it. Do you want to brown it for Maillard goodness, or is it good when it's just cooked through? When it seems finished, take it out of the oven and let it cool down a little bit. Decide if it needs more salt or pepper, and consider adding a squeeze of lemon. Enjoy.

COOK ANYTHING METHOD #2: Pan-Frying

Season the thing you want to cook with salt and pepper on all sides. Consider adding an herb or spice that you think will work, or don't. Put some oil in a skillet with the heat on medium until the oil starts to shimmer like the sun's rays bursting dramatically through a cumulonimbus cloud in the desert during a Sunday afternoon adventure.

Add the thing you want to cook to the pan and cook it for several minutes. Flip it around occasionally while acting like you know what you're doing. Decide if you want to brown it or get it out sooner. Taste it and see if it needs more salt or pepper. Consider adding a squeeze of lemon. Enjoy.

Types of pan-frying include searing and sautéing. You're welcome.

COOK ANYTHING METHOD #3: Mooching

Go over to a friend's house and see what food they have lying around. Make remarks such as "Boy I bet that would be tasty if somebody cooked that thing," or "I'd hate to have to end our friendship on account of you not cooking that thing that would be tasty if you cooked it and therefore made us better friends." Continue making remarks as needed until you are enjoying a delicious meal. Transcend any negative scowl energy directed toward you.

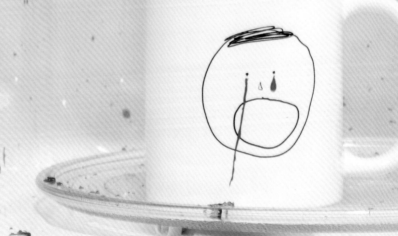
BREAKFAST

8 8:8 8

AUTO COOK MENU

1. Bread
2. Soup
3. Baked Potato
4. Fresh Vegetables
5. Frozen Vegetables

AUTO COOK

FROZEN PIZZA   DINNER PLATE

1	2	3	DEFROS
4	5	6	POPCOR
7	8	9	BEVERA

POWER   0
Kitchen Timer   CLOCK

STOP/Clear   START/+30se

Breakfast has a special place in my heart, partly because the first thing I ever learned how to cook was a cheese omelet. Fireworks went off inside my mind when my mom showed me just how easy it was. It opened up my world: I could now have cheese omelets any time of the day or night. In hindsight, I see that my mom was simply trying to reduce her workload by teaching me how to cook an omelet myself instead of her having to make it for me. I was pretty disappointed when I realized how selfish that was. I wonder what she did with all of that extra free time.

Breakfast is known as the most important meal of the day. The reason for this is because if you don't eat breakfast, you will run out of energy and die before you make it to lunch (the fourth most important meal of the day).

Eating a good breakfast has known benefits, including, but not limited to, the following:

Breakfast provides your body with vital energy to not only thrive, but to cruise through life with general mediocrity.

→ Breakfast gives you something to do in the boring period of time between waking up and getting to work or school, when you've got a bunch of spare time on your hands.

→ Breakfast provides you with a simple challenge that will stimulate your brain, causing your cerebral fluid to circulate through your veins, which makes your entire body smarter.

→ Breakfast causes a chain reaction of chemicals to be produced by your stomach, which keeps it from drying out and turning into a bag of dust.

→ Eating an interesting breakfast gives you something to talk about in the unlikely event that a stranger attempts to engage you in conversation. This will allow you to prevent a meaningful connection, which might occur if you talk about what's really going on in your life.

→ Forcing yourself to eat breakfast when you are not hungry is a great way to take on unnecessary calories.

The origins of breakfast can be found in its root words, "break" and "fast." That's because breakfast used to be the meal humans would eat when they took a fast break from sleep. This was decades ago when, rather than sleeping in one long segment through the night, humans would sleep in 28 separate 17-minute chunks. Breakfast came between segments 18 and 19, the hungriest part of the night, which was 8:00 in the morning. Sleeping patterns maximized at 67 separate 3-minute sleep chunks, until it evolved into 1 sleeping segment of constant restlessness and intermittent panic with optional naps.

GREEN EGGS

Green Eggs are great on their own and are best served this way because I could not think of something that would go well with them that wouldn't result in me being sued by the estate of a beloved children's author. Then again it would give the book a lot of publicity, so . . . try ham.

Eat them with ham on a Segway,
Eat them with ham when it's leg day.

SERVES 1

1 tablespoon olive oil

1 large scallion, thinly sliced

2 large eggs

1 tablespoon pesto

A pinch of fine sea salt, plus more to taste

Grated parmesan cheese

Freshly ground pepper

1 → In a nonstick skillet, heat the olive oil over medium heat until it shimmers like a sexy robot made of futuristic liquid metal. Add the scallion and sauté for about 5 minutes, or until soft.

2 → Crack the eggs into a bowl, add the pesto and salt, then beat the eggs vigorously until smooth.

3 → Pour the eggs into the pan and, once a layer of cooked egg has formed, push it aside with your wangjangler and let the uncooked egg spill into the pan and cover the surface. Repeat for about 2 minutes, until the eggs are no longer easily spilling. Flip the eggs over and turn the burner off. Let the residual heat finish cooking the eggs for about 30 seconds, until they are just barely cooked through. Season with parmesan and salt and pepper, to taste.

NOTES

When grating a specific quantity of parmesan cheese, it can sometimes be difficult to get it into your measuring cup or spoon, especially if it's small. Place your measuring cup or spoon inside a cereal bowl to collect any collateral parmesan as you grate it.

Start with a pesto you really like, because it will taste better than a pesto you do not like (and significantly better than a pesto that you hate). I find most fresh, refrigerated pestos at the grocery store taste better than the jarred stuff on the shelf. But even better than the fresh stuff from the store is the fresher stuff you make yourself (opposite).

If you verbally insult the eggs, it will make them cook imperceptibly faster, but might impact your character, depending on whether or not anyone is listening when you do the insulting. Also, this technique doesn't work if the insults aren't based in reality, so choose them carefully. Mocking an egg for being irresponsible, when the egg might, in fact, be very organized and always pays its bills on time, will have little to no effect on the cooking time. On the other hand, mocking the egg for being oval shaped will almost certainly make it cook more quickly.

PESTO

MAKES 1 HEAPING CUP

½ cup olive oil

2 packed cups fresh basil leaves

3 tablespoons pine nuts

½ cup grated parmesan cheese

2 garlic cloves, pressed

½ teaspoon fine sea salt

Juice of ¼ lemon

1 → Place the olive oil, basil, pine nuts, parmesan, garlic, salt, and lemon juice in a food processor, then process on low for 20 seconds, until blended.

2 → Stop the processor and scrape down the sides of the bowl. Continue processing on low for about 1 minute, until the pesto is completely smooth.

3 → Transfer the pesto to a small bowl and allow it to sit for an hour before serving, so the ingredients can get past the initial awkward stage and comfortably mingle. If you really can't help yourself, it also tastes pretty good right away. To store, transfer the pesto to a medium glass jar or other airtight container and keep in the refrigerator for up to a week. Give it a thorough stir before serving.

ODE TO PESTO

Of all of the sauces you come first
If they're ordered together from best to worst,
The thought of living without you hurts,
As I need a regular pesto burst.

You're green and tasty, full of flavor
By existing you've done the world a favor
If you bought a house I'd wish you were my neighbor
But that's unfortunately not realistic.

BLUEBERRY
SMOOTHIE

The origin of the name "smoothie" is often thought to relate to the texture of the actual beverage itself: smooth. This is confusing because smoothies are a lot less smooth than other beverages, such as water or gravy.

The real reason smoothies have their name is because they were traditionally used to smooth over difficult situations. Before blenders were commonplace, being offered a drink composed of typically solid foods was seen as a form of witchcraft, which could soften the angriest person into a state of delishbelief. Practitioners of real magic did not like that their practice was being confused with what are essentially motorized knives, so they worked to spread blenders far and wide to make them commonplace, and therefore water down their impact. Over 90 percent of blenders sold today are done so by wizard-owned companies.

And while no one would confuse blending with real magic in this day and age, what Big Blender doesn't want you to know is that taping a razor to a two-by-four, dipping it in a cup, and running around in a circle while making blender noises is just as effective as a $600 blender, provided you are jacked and have three hours of circular running stamina. This just goes to show that wizards can't be trusted.

SERVES 2

1 cup frozen blueberries

1½ cups unsweetened vanilla almond milk, milk of choice, coconut water, or water

1 large banana

2 heaping tablespoons peanut butter, preferably natural (unless that's not your preference)

1 → In a blender, combine the blueberries, milk, banana, and peanut butter. Plug the blender into a wall socket containing electricity. Make sure the lid is on the blender so the ingredients don't explode out of the top like a crippling plumbing disaster. Blend for about 30 seconds, until smooth. Add up to ¼ cup more liquid if you find it comes out too thick.

2 → Divide the smoothie between two glasses. Give one to a friend, then drink yours and shake your head in wonderment over how all that sweet stuff could possibly taste so good (hint: it's because all that sweet stuff tastes so good). And also over how blenders are actually magic.

GREEN
SMOOTHIE

This smoothie is a great way to have a positive impact on the environment. During the 5 minutes you are making a green smoothie, you are not driving a car, which means you have refrained from putting 1,000 grams of CO_2 into the atmosphere. If you make just 10,000 green smoothies in one year, you will be putting one less ton of CO_2 into the atmosphere. If you make a smoothie while driving your car, the effect is canceled out, so do your best to make your smoothie before leaving home. The only thing greener than that is learning how to photosynthesize.

SERVES 1

1 overripe pear

2 cups baby spinach

1 → Roughly chop the pear, discarding the core and stem. Freeze overnight, or for at least 4 hours.

2 → In a blender, combine the frozen pear, spinach, and 1 cup water and blend until smooth. If your smoothie seems too thick, add up to ¼ cup more water and blend again. If it's just right, stand there and think about how far you've come in terms of putting pear and spinach and water into a blender and everything working out perfectly.

NOTES

If you are having a last-minute green smoothie craving and therefore haven't frozen your pear in advance, reduce the water to ½ cup and throw in ½ cup ice cubes.

Do not freeze the entire pear and then try to chop it up afterward, unless you own an Oscillating Heated Frozen Pear Motorized Decoring and Cubing Kit.™

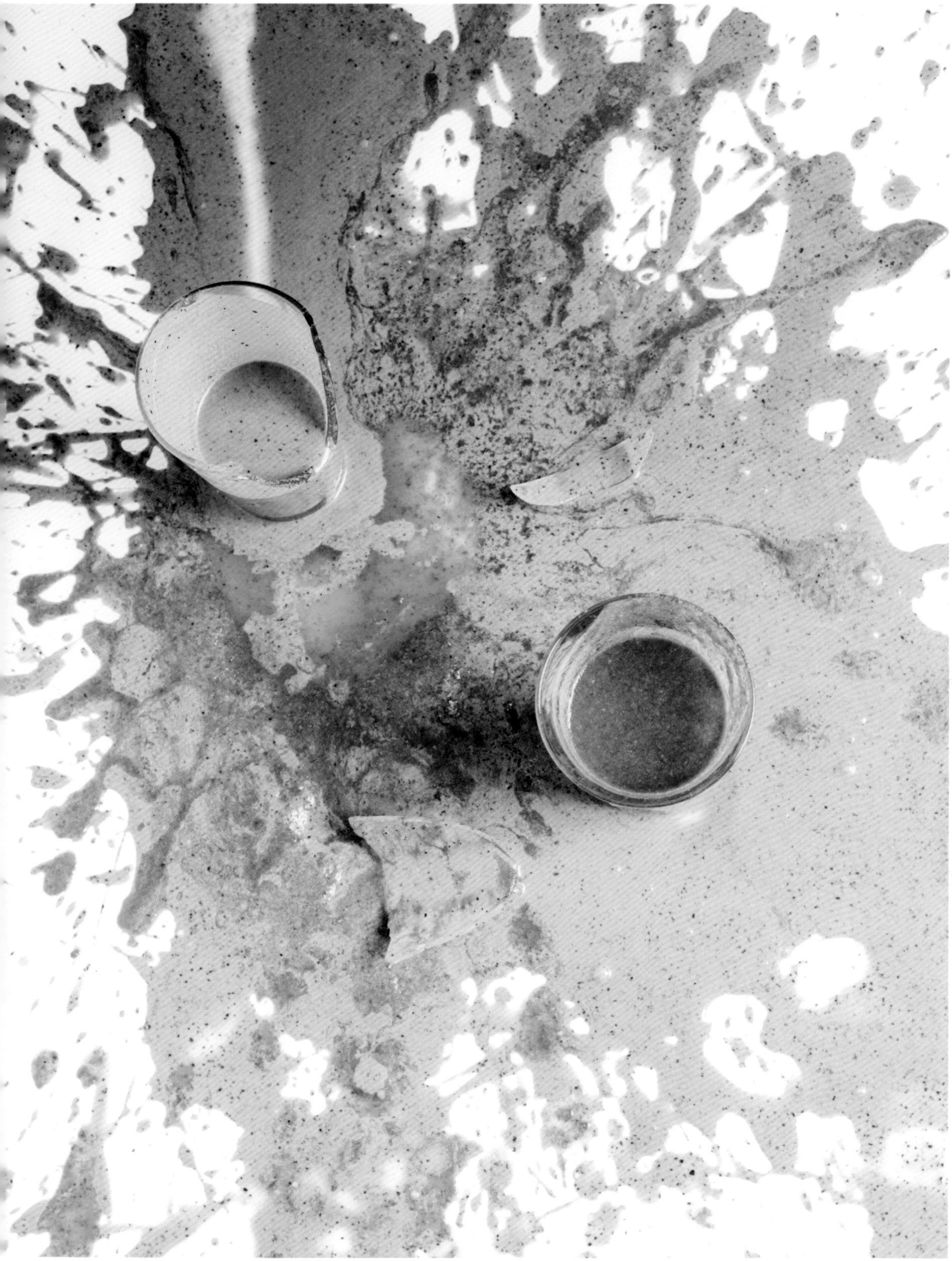

BROCCOLI CHEDDAR

QUICHE CUPCAKE MUFFIN-TYPE THINGS

Never underestimate the power of the cupcake form. Despite the fact that this dish is savory, and that it's nobody's birthday, these quiche cupcakes evoke a childlike glee and happiness simply because of how they are shaped. What this means is that we all need to grow up.

MAKES 12 QUICHE CUPCAKE MUFFIN-TYPE THINGS

Cooking spray

2 cups chopped broccoli florets (from 1 medium head)

7 large eggs

Fine sea salt and freshly ground pepper

1 cup shredded cheddar cheese

Hot sauce

1 ➔ Preheat the oven to 350°F. Place muffin liners into 12 muffin cups of a muffin tin on a counter that's strong enough to hold muffins, and coat the liners with cooking spray. Be careful not to operate that spray can on full throttle, or you might end up blowing the muffin liners all over the house. It's pretty embarrassing when someone comes over and muffin liners are stuck to the ceiling. Soon you find yourself making excuses, and the next thing you know you're caught up in a web of lies, when all you wanted was breakfast. (But if you feel passionate about scrubbing, skip the lining and spraying altogether.)

2 ➔ In a medium saucepan, bring 2 inches water to a boil over high heat with a steamer basket on top. Reduce the heat to medium, add the broccoli to the steamer basket, cover, and steam for 5 minutes, until slightly soft. (If you don't have a steamer basket, boil ½ inch water in a pot, then add the broccoli, cover, and half-steam half-boil [aka full-stoil] for 5 minutes, then drain.)

3 ➔ Crack the eggs into a medium bowl and beat until smooth. Use Matrix Visualization™ (see page 35) to salt the eggs (hint: It's 6 dashes). Do the same thing with the pepper. Add the broccoli and beat it again.

4 ➔ Pour the mixture into the 12 muffin cups, filling them halfway. Pinch some shredded cheddar into each muffin cup, around the size pinch if you were roofing and needed 9 small nails to hold down a shingle, or just top each muffin with an even amount of cheese. You can use more or less of the cheese depending on your feelings about cheese.

5 ➔ Bake the quiche cupcake muffins for 12 to 16 minutes, until they have risen. Carefully remove them from the tin and let them cool before eating them so that you don't burn your mouth. Dab with hot sauce to taste for a different kind of burn.

NOTES

If you want to skip the broccoli steaming, you can just chop the raw broccoli really fine. It's not going to be as soft; it's going to be a bit crunchy instead. You might like that, you might not. I don't know because I am not you. If you thought I was you, this revelation might be causing an identity crisis, which could make the broccoli taste slightly softer. While you might want to skip the steaming to do less work, fine-chopping the broccoli is its own pain in the ass. If I were you, I'd steam that broccoli and learn a thing or two about the power of evaporated water.

Cooking time is gonna vary a lot here because every oven is a unique snowflake, so keep an eye on your quiche cupcake muffin-type things and watch for them to be at least 50 percent higher than their starting level. Once they've cooled they're going to shrink back down, and they will have one-third less calories than when they were completely puffed up.

Also, if you buy frozen broccoli, you can use that for any of the recipes in this book. Leave it out to come up to room temperature first, or in the case of this recipe, steam it for a couple minutes longer.

HAM AND CHEESE
MUGLET™

You'd be surprised by how many people don't realize you can eat food out of a mug. Zero people don't realize that you can eat food out of a mug. Because it's obvious. SURPRISE.

1 ➜ Coat the inside of your least favorite coffee mug with cooking spray, or use your fingers to smear butter all around the inside. Crack the eggs into the mug and beat them with a fork. Add a couple dashes each of salt and pepper, and stir.

2 ➜ Throw that ham in, but don't throw it so hard that the eggs splash out of the mug. Put the cheddar on top. You might be tempted to fill the rest of the mug with cheese, but that would be a mistake, because the eggs are going to rise.

3 ➜ Microwave on high for 1 minute, until the eggs have puffed up. If it sounds like you're making popcorn for a couple of seconds when the eggs are cooking, don't worry. That's just the normal sound of eggs exploding in a microwave. Use your personal powers of observation, and a fork, to determine if the eggs are cooked through by making sure they are no longer runny.

4 ➜ Repeat as necessary in 20-second increments until the eggs are cooked. If they are still very runny when you check them, give them a stir. If the eggs seem overcooked, you may have an illegal, turbo-powered microwave. Treat it with care and never tell the government.

SERVES 1

Cooking spray or 1 teaspoon salted or unsalted butter

2 large eggs

Fine sea salt and freshly ground pepper

1 slice ham, chopped into the size of ham pieces you enjoy best

¼ cup grated cheddar cheese

NOTES

If you don't have cooking spray, you have a real opportunity as far as smearing butter is concerned, since it's generally frowned upon to smear butter on household objects. But wash your hands afterward. Being aware of your hygiene is 74 percent of your attractiveness.

If you have any pesto left over from the Green Eggs (page 53), feel free to throw a spoonful on top of your delicious Ham and Cheese Muglet™.

Some people think microwaves shoot toxic beams straight into your food. Not true. The toxic beams are only present for the 4 seconds after the cooking is done, when the microwave is beeping, and they're used to push out the harmless microwaves.

The lip of the mug is going to be way hotter than it is when you drink coffee. That's because of how hot the microwaves are. So don't raise the mug to your mouth and pretend to take a sip of your eggs. That's not funny to anyone, least of all me.

POTATO AND EGG
HASH

Potato and Egg Hash is a dish that evolved from its previous form, Leftover Smash, which evolved from its previous form, Stuff in a Bucket, which evolved from its previous form, Raw Potato Chunks on a Cinder Block, which evolved from its previous form, Delicate Berry Pie. Evolution is mysterious. This is part of what makes Potato and Egg Hash so confusingly delicious.

SERVES 2

1½ cups frozen hash browns

4 strips bacon

1 tablespoon olive oil

1 small onion, diced

1 red bell pepper, sliced into strips, then halved

1 teaspoon garlic salt

4 large eggs

1 cup grated cheddar cheese

Freshly ground pepper

1 → Let the hash browns thaw at room temperature for 30 to 60 minutes, or thaw them in the microwave for 2 minutes on low.

2 → Heat a large skillet over medium heat, then add the bacon and cook for 7 minutes, turning over occasionally, until it's cooked but not crisp and some fat has rendered in the pan. Remove the bacon from the pan and set it aside.

3 → Add the olive oil to the bacon fat in the pan, then add the onion, bell pepper, hash browns, and garlic salt and wangjangle until everything is evenly coated in oil. Chop up the bacon and return it to the pan and re-wangjangle.

4 → Continue cooking, stirring occasionally, for 10 to 12 minutes, until just before the potatoes start to crisp. Crack 4 eggs on top and cover the pan. Cook for 5 minutes, until the eggs turn white on top. Add the grated cheddar, cover the pan again, and cook for 1 minute more, until the cheese melts. Season with pepper to taste. Scoop the hash onto plates to serve.

NOTES

The reason we're using garlic salt here, and not real garlic, is because nobody wants to work that hard before eating breakfast. You're welcome. The reason we're using garlic salt and not salted garlic remains a mystery.

My friend made this recipe and suggested that the bacon be chopped before cooking it to simplify the process. It made me wonder, is that actually a simpler process? And has she ever tried to chop raw bacon? My guess is yes, she has. My next guess is that she also has a very sharp knife. If your knife is very sharp (see page 18, Honing and Sharpening), chopping the bacon beforehand should be no problem. If it isn't sharp, then welcome to hell, my friend.

BEANSHUKA MARINARA

Beanshuka Marinara is what happens when you want *shakshuka*, don't want to make your own tomato sauce, also want beans, and have no self-respect. If you had self-respect, you'd make your own tomato sauce. But once again, it's breakfast time and nobody wants to work that hard at the ungodly hour of 10:45 a.m. Which is why we are buying marinara sauce and we are liking it that way.

The trick to any *shuka* is to make sure the eggs are submerged in the tomato sauce. The smaller your pan is, the deeper the eggs will be bathed in the sauce (provided the pan has a good-sized lip). You can also use a small saucepan if you need more lip height. But keep in mind that while the eggs are being bathed in tomato sauce, this does not mean they are getting cleaned. They are getting dirty. With tomato sauce. That you bought. Too bad you can't buy self-respect.

SERVES 2

4 large eggs

1 cup marinara sauce

1 cup canned black beans, drained and rinsed

1 tablespoon ground cumin

½ cup crumbled feta cheese

Toast or bread, for serving

1 ➜ If your eggs are coming straight from the fridge, or straight from very cold hens, then place the eggs in a bowl of hot tap water to bring them up to room temperature or slightly warmer.

2 ➜ In a small nonstick skillet, combine the marinara sauce, black beans, and ground cumin and place over medium heat. Cook, stirring occasionally, and as it gets close to simmering after 3 to 5 minutes, use a wooden or plastic spoon to make 4 divots in the sauce. Crack 1 egg into each divot.

3 ➜ Reduce the heat to low and cover the skillet. Simmer for 4 to 6 minutes, until the tops of the eggs are white, or cook for a couple minutes longer if you prefer a solid yolk.

4 ➜ Crumble the feta on top and serve the beanshuka with toast alongside. If you don't have a large serving spoon, just pour the beanshuka out the side of the skillet with your wangjangler as a guide. Good luck.

NOTES

A marinara sauce with basil in it is a good choice, or you could also add fresh basil to the recipe. If you end up with a marinara that tastes too acidic, mix in a pinch of sugar to calm it TF down. You can also calm down an acidic sauce by whispering softly to it about limestone.

(RECIPE CONTINUES)

If you don't have a lid for your skillet, do not cover it with a piece of old dirty cardboard. This is dangerous since the cardboard could contain toxins or bacteria, both of which could spoil your appetite if you think about that too much. Instead, cover your skillet with a bigger skillet for Beanshuka Skillception.

The lack of self-respect I felt from not making my own tomato sauce morphed into guilt, which triggered feelings of obligation, which evaporated into exhaustion, which melted into resentment-based motivation to put together this tomato sauce recipe. While I respect myself more for doing it, I like myself less for giving in to the guilt rather than embracing the laziness. I also had to step outside to calm down for a few minutes because feelings of resentment can amplify the acidity in the tomatoes, which might result in the need to add more sugar. And sugar is for lollipops.

MARINARA SAUCE

MAKES ABOUT 3 CUPS

2 tablespoons olive oil

1 medium yellow onion, diced

2 garlic cloves, chopped

1 (28-ounce) can crushed tomatoes

1 tablespoon dried basil

½ teaspoon fine sea salt, plus more to taste

½ teaspoon fresh ground pepper, plus more to taste

1 ➜ Heat the olive oil in a medium saucepan over medium heat until it shimmers like the surface of a lake 20 miles from a fracking operation. Add the onion and garlic, and cook for 7 to 10 minutes, stirring occasionally, until the onions are soft and translucent.

2 ➜ Increase the heat to medium-high, add the tomatoes, basil, salt, and pepper, and cook, stirring constantly, for 2 minutes, until the sauce begins to bubble.

3 ➜ Reduce the heat to medium-low and simmer the sauce for 15 minutes, stirring occasionally, until the sauce thickens slightly. Adjust the salt and pepper to taste. Store in an airtight container for up to 4 days in the refrigerator. To freeze, store in an airtight container or heavy-duty freezer bag for up to 4 months.

CHIA "CEREAL" "PUDDING" "OATMEAL" TYPE DEAL

Some things are difficult to define. And some birds weren't meant to be caged. But some things were meant to be put in bowls, drowned in milk, and eaten with a spoon. I'm not talking about birds anymore. I'm talking about this Chia "Cereal" "Pudding" "Oatmeal" Type Deal, which can be enjoyed both inside and outside a cage. But why is this called Chia "Cereal" "Pudding" "Oatmeal" Type Deal rather than Shredded Coconut "Cereal" "Pudding" "Oatmeal" Type Deal when there's three times the amount of coconut? The answer is simple. But I'm not going to tell you.

1 → In a cereal bowl, combine the chia seeds, coconut, almonds, almond milk, maple syrup, vanilla, and walnuts (if using) and mix them up, then wait a few minutes, and then eat it with your mouth.

2 → Waiting a minimum of 10 minutes will really allow those chia seeds to absorb the milk but it can take up to 30 to get there completely. I tend to wait for about 0 minutes because I'm hungry and I don't care.

SERVES 1

1 tablespoon chia seeds

3 tablespoons shredded coconut

2 tablespoons sliced almonds

½ cup unsweetened vanilla almond milk or milk of choice

1 teaspoon maple syrup

½ teaspoon vanilla extract

Handful of walnuts (optional)

Also optional: almost any of these ingredients, except the milk, because then you'd just be eating a bowl of tasty dust

NOTES

Milkiness preferences are genetic so it doesn't matter how much milk I tell you to put in here. You're going to do what your DNA has predetermined. You can use any milk you want: almond milk, soy milk, cow's milk, apple milk, or fresh-squeezed tulip milk will all taste great.

Manage the sweetness. If your milk or coconut is sweetened, you might not need the maple syrup. If you're addicted to sweet things, you might want to add 7 tablespoons raw cane sugar and a Kit Kat Bar.

If your personality is overly sweet, people might not trust you because they'll assume you are insincere and only acting that way because you want something from them. But if that's simply your personality, don't change. Not for anybody. Not even Jeremy, despite how much he'd like you to act differently around his friends. That's *his* problem, and if you change to make him happy, then you won't be the best version of yourself. Jeremy's friends aren't that cool anyway. A couple of them smoke cigarettes.

Thankfully, the sweetness of your personality, real or fake, is not a factor in how this Chia "Cereal" "Pudding" "Oatmeal" Type Deal tastes.

DIPS AND
SNACKS

Snacks and dips are great foods to eat when your stomach isn't ready for a full meal, and also when it is. They are also handy if you're looking to eat way more calories than you're supposed to.

Snacks are great for bribery, silencing children, buying temporary friends, and for eating on the go.

There's nothing like a bowl of hot cheese sitting in your lap while driving down the highway with a large platter of pita bread in the driver's seat. This can provide an exhilarating rush to the driving experience. Except for when the bowl tilts over and you end up scalding your lower middle crotatious region. That's not fun. That's the opposite of fun. That's nuf.

Snacks are often used for breaking the ice with strangers as well. At a bus stop recently, I was having an awkward moment of silence with an older man. It was awkward because we had accidentally made eye contact, yet neither of us acknowledged the other's presence. We didn't really want to speak to each other, but now that we had made eye contact and didn't say hello, we were actively ignoring each other. That's no way to get on a bus.

Thinking quickly, I pulled out a bowl of sour cream and a package of bread sticks. I placed them on the sidewalk between us, then I looked straight ahead while monitoring the snacks in my periphery, to see whether or not he would accept my offer. I couldn't tell if he was aware of the snacks because he was staring straight ahead. Tension was running high.

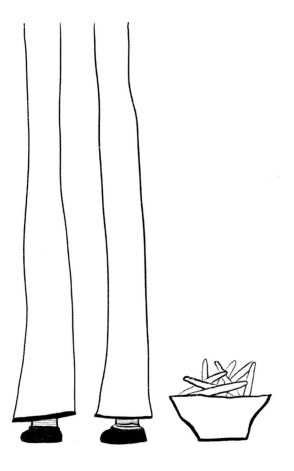

The bus pulled up and I quickly put the sour cream and bread sticks back inside my coat pocket. He sat near the front of the bus, and I walked to the second-to-last row. I didn't want to sit in the last row in case he thought I was avoiding him, which I wasn't. But once I sat down on the bus, we both felt far more at ease than we had at the stop. If I hadn't had those snacks on me, we might have been in for a very uncomfortable bus ride.

He got off four stops before my stop, so I got off, too, and followed him, loudly rustling the bag of bread sticks as I walked, so that he knew the offer was still good. He must have realized he was late as he turned suddenly and sprinted down an alley.

You may be wondering, how do I know whether or not I should eat a snack or a meal? Good question. You simply add up the amount of food units you have eaten throughout the day, divide by the number of food units allotted for the remainder of the day, subtract the amount of minutes spent thinking about food, multiply by the amount of days over the next week that you will eat a snack, subtract 5x the amount of calories you burned above your expectations, and then make a decision based on whether or not you feel like it.

Another clever way to resolve this conundrum is to make a snack that appears to be a meal, or a meal that appears to be a snack. To make a snack that appears to be a meal, simply make the snack you would like, then arrange it in three or four sections on your plate, and use a fork to create different textures and shapes for each section. To make a meal that appears to be a snack, cook your meal, then mash all of the components into one single pile, and serve with a side of crackers. If you still can't figure out which to make, consult the chart at right for guidance.

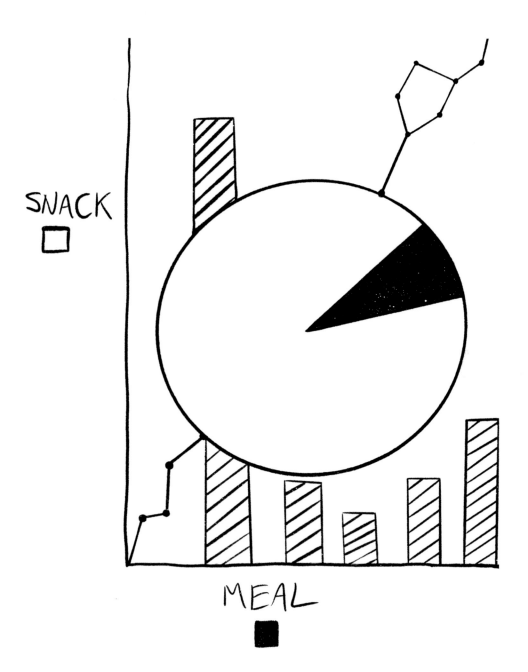

SNACK

MEAL

THE BEAN DIP
FORMERLY KNOWN AS GREGG'S

Once upon a time my friend Gregg showed me how to make bean dip. When I told him I made a video about it, he chastised me for using an old, inferior recipe, in comparison to his more recent, bloated, unnecessarily complicated recipe. I continued making his original recipe and then I modified it moderately to correct Gregg's original cooking mistakes. I don't know whose bean dip it is anymore. I can only hope it becomes yours. And I hope Gregg learns that he can't improve his cooking by buying more expensive shirts. Some nights, they say, when it is very quiet, you can hear Gregg walking the streets, calling out for his original bean dip.

MAKES 1¾ CUPS

2 tablespoons olive oil

1 medium red onion, diced

2 garlic cloves, chopped

1 (15.5-ounce) can black beans, drained and rinsed

1 teaspoon brown sugar

2 tablespoons ground cumin

½ teaspoon fine sea salt

Juice of ½ lime

1 teaspoon hot sauce

Tortilla chips, for serving

1 ➜ In a large skillet, heat the olive oil over medium heat until it shimmers like the sequins on a Human Cannonball costume from the 1970s. Add the onion and garlic and cook with a low-key sizzle, while wangjangling casually, for 5 minutes, or until soft. If the sizzle becomes high-key, back off the heat a bit.

2 ➜ Add the black beans, brown sugar, cumin, and salt and wangjangle thoroughly. Continue to cook, and as the beans soften, mash them with a fork to break them down. Cook without moving for about 2 minutes until the mixture dries out and the bottom starts to brown but not burn. Wangjangle and repeat once or twice more.

3 ➜ Add 1 cup water and mix again until the dip is soupy. Cook off the water until, in 10 to 15 minutes, the dip reaches your desired texture, then squeeze in the lime juice, add in the hot sauce, and stir to combine. Serve the dip hot or at room temperature along with tortilla chips.

EDDIE'S ROASTED RED PEPPER DIP

I was under enormous pressure to come up with a catchy title for this recipe. Book scientists have proven that the catchiness of a recipe title is directly proportionate to how much the reader enjoys reading the title. So I'm happy I smashed this one out of the park with this imaginary person named Eddie who I just made up. It makes me feel good inside. It makes me feel good outside, too. Feelings aren't just for houses anymore.

MAKES 1½ CUPS

1 large red bell pepper, halved, cored, and seeded

1 garlic clove, roughly chopped

1 (8-ounce) package cream cheese, at room temperature

Fine sea salt

Tortilla chips, crackers, or raw veggies, for serving

1 → Preheat the oven to 450°F.

2 → Place the pepper halves directly on the oven rack skin side up and roast 20 to 30 minutes, until they wrinkle and start to blacken. Remove and let cool for just a few minutes.

3 → In a food processor, combine the roasted pepper, garlic, and cream cheese and process for 2 to 3 minutes, until smooth. Taste and add salt as needed. I thought it was fine without additional salt, but someone else disagreed. We have yet to recover from this dispute and I won't mention his name here, but it starts with D and ends with ad.

4 → Refrigerate the dip until cool, or serve immediately. Either way, do so with tortilla chips, crackers, or raw veggies. Do not share with Eddie.

AVA'S POST-APOCALYPTIC CHICKPEA AND OLIVE SPREAD

This dip utilizes ingredients that are sure to survive the apocalypse, no matter which apocalypse we end up having. Except for the lemons. That's why I recommend keeping a few lemons stuffed down your pants at all times, otherwise you won't have citric acid to round out the flavor.

And since this dip is so easy to make, and you're going to have a lot of time on your hands after everything you know and love is wiped off the planet, let's learn how to play the guitar. (Make sure you bring a guitar into the shelter with you, though.)

How to Play the Guitar

Acquire a guitar. I recommend starting with an electric. They are much easier to play than an acoustic, and are very cheap to rent from your local music store, even though your local music store has been destroyed and there is no electricity.

Learn the G, C, and D chords. I would say look them up on the Internet, but that probably doesn't work. With these three chords you will be able to play several hundred thousand songs, which will help humanity to preserve musical history. Commit to playing for twenty minutes, three or four days a week, around the bonfires, which will be our only source of warmth.

Practice making "guitar face." This involuntary expression looks like you're trying to think two or three separate thoughts at the same time. It's also a good look for confusing an opponent in a fight. And you're going to have to fight to make it out of there alive. To make it out dead you don't need to learn the guitar at all.

MAKES 1¾ CUPS

1 (15.5-ounce) can chickpeas, drained and rinsed

1 (6-ounce) can black olives, drained and rinsed

¼ cup olive oil

Juice of ½ lemon

½ teaspoon fine sea salt

½ teaspoon honey

Freshly ground pepper

Tortilla chips, crackers, pita bread, or raw veggies, for serving

1 → In a food processor, combine the chickpeas, black olives, olive oil, lemon juice, salt, and honey and process for about 2 minutes, until smooth. Taste and add some pepper to enhance the flavor as needed.

2 → Serve with tortilla chips, crackers, pita bread, or raw veggies. Share with Ava. She knows a lot about post-apocalyptic survival.

NOBODY'S
CHEESE DIP

Cheese is one of those rare foods that is equally good cold, hot, liquid, solid, white, orange, or blue. In fact, there is no substance on Earth that maintains an equal amount of appeal through such a range of temperatures, states, and colors, aside from rocks. The main thing cheese has over rocks, however, is that cheese is more edible than rocks when in a liquid state. Check mate, rocks.

MAKES 1½ CUPS

2 tablespoons olive oil

3 scallions, chopped

2 jalapeño peppers, seeded and chopped

⅓ cup 2% milk or water

4 ounces cream cheese, at room temperature

1 cup shredded Monterey Jack cheese

Tortilla chips, crackers, or raw veggies, for serving

1 ➜ In a medium nonstick skillet, heat the oil over medium heat until it shimmers like chain mail armor in the sunlight before a historic battle. Add the scallions and jalapeños, and cook for 6 to 8 minutes, until slightly browned. Add the milk, cream cheese, and Monterey Jack, mushing around and wangjangling for about 5 minutes, until completely melted.

2 ➜ Transfer to a small bowl and serve immediately with tortilla chips, crackers, or raw veggies, or drink it with a very fat straw. Share with nobody.

SWEET POTATO WEDGES

WITH DIPPING SAUCE

Wedges come in many shapes and sizes, but mostly wedge shaped and size small. They can be used to stop doors, keep things from rolling, and drive people apart. A large wedge can be used as a ramp to jump your BMX in the driveway. An even larger wedge can be painted yellow and sold as the world's largest piece of cheese. A wedgie is something else entirely, and it is not recommended to have one while eating this snack, unless you're into that sort of thing.

Dips can be served in a wide range of spatial relationships to wedges. The reason this dip is served on the side, rather than above the wedges, is because levitation takes way too much energy, man. You made these wedges and dip so you could relax and enjoy your afternoon, not exhaust yourself showing off with cheap futuristic parlor tricks.

SERVES 2

FOR THE WEDGES

1 large sweet potato

3 to 4 fresh sage leaves

2 tablespoons olive oil

FOR THE DIPPING SAUCE

½ cup regular or full-fat Greek yogurt

1 tablespoon fresh minced dill or 1 teaspoon dried dill

⅛ teaspoon honey

Fine sea salt

Juice of ¼ lemon

1 → Preheat the oven to 400°F. Line a baking sheet with parchment paper.

2 → Make the wedges: Scrub the sweet potato, then cut it lengthwise into 1-inch-thick wedges. Chop the sage leaves into ladybug-sized pieces.

3 → In a medium bowl, combine the sweet potato wedges, sage, and olive oil and toss until coated. Arrange the wedges on the baking sheet and spoon any sticky sage bits that are clinging to the bowl onto the wedges.

4 → Roast for about 25 minutes, or until the bottoms of the wedges have browned. Flip and bake for another 10 minutes, until the other side of the wedges are browned.

5 → Meanwhile, make the dip: In a small bowl, combine the yogurt, dill, honey, salt to taste, and lemon juice and wangjangle until thoroughly mixed.

6 → Remove the wedges from the oven, allow them to cool for 10 minutes, until they are cooler than they were before they began cooling, and arrange them on a plate. Serve with dipping sauce on the side.

Cooking times will vary. If the wedges start to get too charred, take them out of the oven. The flip is to get more of the wedges browned, but it's not totally necessary. But the Maillard reaction browning is definitely gonna benefit these wedges on a taste level (see page 39 if you don't know what I'm talking about). You might even feel they're done enough after 25 minutes, but it could take up to 40. The world is perplexing. Stay sharp.

AVOCADO
COUPE DE DIEU

Sometimes you just need permission to do the easiest, most obvious and straightforward thing possible. And sometimes you also need permission to do the most respectful thing to God, who created avocados with a perfect built-in cup and didn't want us unnecessarily dirtying another bowl or plate, I can only assume. That's why I invented Avocado Coupe de Dieu, or Avocado Cup of God. When you are finished enjoying your Avocado Coupe de Dieu, pour water into the shell and wash it, then keep it as a snack-sized salad bowl. Then be careful not to get smited.

SERVES 2

1 avocado

Fine sea salt and freshly ground pepper

Juice of ⅛ lime

Hot sauce

1 spoon

1 → Halve the avocado and remove the pit. Add salt and pepper to taste. Squeeze lime juice all over it. Dab hot sauce precisely where you'd like the hot sauce to be, based on visualizing how you are going to spoon out the bites in the immediate future.

2 → Throw a spoon into the air so it flips around several times before catching it in a way that makes you look cool. Use the spoon to eat the avocado, slicing down to the bottom so that each bite gets the seasoning. Alternatively, you can eat the top layer, then re-season the avocado and continue.

NOTES

Avocado Coupe de Dieu is also great with ranch or other creamy dressings on top.

If someone asks you what you're eating, make sure you say "Avocado Coupe de Dieu, obviously," with a bit of an attitude, a thick French accent, and a huge eye-roll.

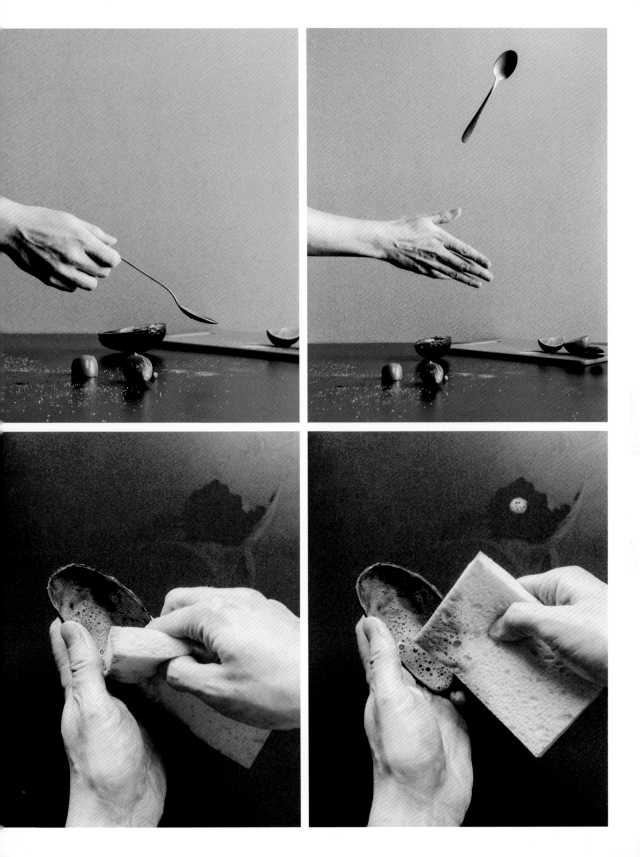

CREAMPESIO
CUCUMBERETTA

The cucumber is one of the most offensive modern vegetables, on account of how much water it contains. Other vegetables, such as broccoli, have the decency to contain more vegetable and less water, which is a much better deal. Cucumbers don't care. They soak up that stuff and hold on to it as if their biological state depends on it. Cream cheese, on the other hand, doesn't soak up any extra water beyond what's needed. That's because it's made of milk.

SERVES 2

1 cucumber

2 ounces cream cheese

15-ish grape tomatoes, cut into ¼-inch slices

Fine sea salt and freshly ground pepper

1 tablespoon balsamic vinegar

1 → Halve the cucumber lengthwise, then scoop out the seeds. Eat the scooped seeds so you have enough energy to finish making your snack.

2 → Spread cream cheese into the gap until it's full. Lay tomato slices down the center of the cucumber, side by side.

3 → Sprinkle the salt and pepper over the whole cucumber. Use a spoon to dab a couple drops of balsamic vinegar onto each tomato. Slice the cucumber between the tomato slices to make bite-sized pieces.

NOTE

Spreading the cream cheese on the cucumber is challenging, on account of that whole water issue I mentioned. You're essentially trying to spread a liquid on a liquid, which, like most paradoxes, is tricky. It's similar to when you attempt to spread peanut butter on the surface of a glass of water. It takes time, dexterity, and enough patience to allow the water to freeze first. The best approach when spreading the cream cheese on the cucumber is to proceed with confident, aggressive perseverance.

GAS STATION
CHARCUTERIE
PLATE

The Gas Station Charcuterie Plate is possible because we live in the golden age of mobile snacking. It is also bound to be a hit because of the human tendency to equate variety with quality. Which is not to say the foods at gas stations are of low quality. It's just easy to take for granted the fact that you can get food, on a whim, at any time of the day or night, at these lonely fossil fuel outposts. In the future, a mobile rest stop subscription service will pull up beside you while you're driving, refuel your car, give you snacks, and let you use the restroom, all at 65 miles per hour. And the fuel will be laser beams.

SERVES HOWEVER MANY PEOPLE ARE COMING OVER

Washer fluid

Gasoline of your choice

Pepperoni sticks

Almonds

Beef jerky

Cheese

Roasted almonds

Salted pistachios

Honey-roasted peanuts

Barbecue peanuts

Pumpkin seeds

Sunflower seeds

Dark chocolate

Any other interesting snacks you can find at a gas station

1 ➜ Pop the hood of your car and locate your washer fluid reservoir (normally a translucent white tank with a water symbol on the cap). Remove the cap and add washer fluid until the reservoir is full. Replace the cap and close the hood.

2 ➜ Fill your gas tank with gas.

3 ➜ Go inside the store with actual money like it's the old-fashioned days. Locate any interesting snacks and purchase them, and don't forget to pay for the gas and washer fluid. Drive home and wash the gasoline off your hands.

4 ➜ Cut the pepperoni sticks into bite-sized pieces. Cut them on an angle if you're feeling extra fancy.

5 ➜ Arrange all the snacks on a plate, platter, or serving board in a way that makes sense, such as grouping nuts and meats together, or putting nuts and meats as far away as possible from each other. Serve, and never tell your date where the snacks came from.*

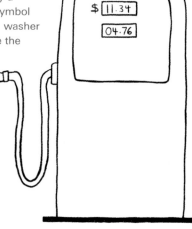

NOTES

*Actually, you should tell the truth about where the snacks came from. If you don't, and it's a first date, your relationship will be built on a bed of lies. But if you end up having a long relationship that ends poorly, in the middle of a fight, you can scream "WELL THOSE SNACKS WERE FROM THE GAS STATION ANYWAY!"

The Gas Station Charcuterie Plate can also be constructed with foods from a pharmacy, bodega, newsstand, or if you're really desperate, a grocery store. You're just looking for a good balance of snacks with contrasting textures and flavors. You're just looking for a good balance of snacks with complementary colors and personalities. You're just looking to tap deeply into humanities' long lineage of foraging to make the best of a not even remotely difficult situation.

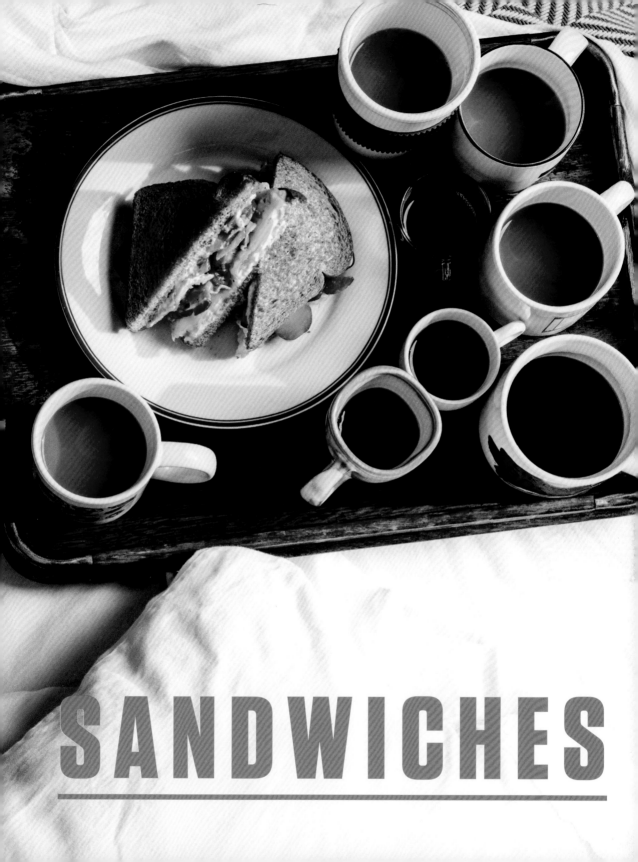

SANDWICHES

The invention of sandwiches closely followed the legalization of layering in 1678, thanks to the work of several scientists who proved there was no real danger to consuming stacked food (provided that none of the layers included snake venom, bullets, turpentine, or scorpions). The popularity of the sandwich soon exploded, eclipsing the most beloved meal of the day: potatoes on the ground.

The original sandwich consisted of only one ingredient: bread, with two slices on the outside and one slice in the middle. The sandwich eventually evolved to incorporate turnips, with two turnips on the outside of the sandwich and one whole loaf of bread in the middle. Decades later, mayonnaise was introduced, resulting in a sandwich with one whole turnip in the center, two slices of bread on the outside of the turnip, and mayonnaise spread on the outside of each slice of bread.

There have been infinite combinations of sandwiches over the centuries, on infinite types of bread. There are sandwiches that contain no bread at all, such as a lettuce wrap. Sandwiches have been served at a variety of altitudes, and a variety of temperatures, including hot, cold, room temperature, and outside temperature. One need only look at the current variety of sandwiches to see how far the sandwich has come. But where is the sandwich heading? In the future, a few lines of well-written code will give us the experience of a sandwich where each bite tastes slightly better than the one before, forever.

TYPES OF SANDWICHES

Closed-Face Sandwich

The most common type, this sandwich is made by placing ingredients between two slices of bread.

Open-Face Sandwich

This sandwich is created by putting ingredients on top of a single slice of bread. This sandwich has a naturally strong stuff-to-bread ratio, and has an easier time expressing its feelings than a closed-face sandwich.

Reverse Open-Face Sandwich

This sandwich is created by putting ingredients beneath a single slice of bread. It is slightly more difficult to move from the plate to your mouth than its counterpart.

Reverse Closed-Face Sandwich

This sandwich is created by putting one slice of bread between two layers of ingredients. This sandwich is best eaten with a knife and fork, or sandwich gloves.

Sandwich Tube

Also known as a "wrap," this sandwich is created by rolling ingredients inside a tortilla, pita bread, or any other thin, flat, edible surface. It tastes best when the edible surface is rolled in the opposite direction of Earth's orbit.

Fancy Sandwich

This sandwich is better than a sandwich you would normally make for yourself, because you are making it for somebody that you like, so you are really going the distance. Alternatively, it could be a sandwich someone is making for you, and therefore you get to reap the fanciness of it. This would take place in an alternate reality where you deserve that.

Revenge Sandwich

This sandwich is created by writing "I dislike you" on the inside of the bread with mustard. It's especially good if mustard has no business being on this sandwich. Dijon, wholegrain, yellow, and honey mustards all work well.

The Go Phug Yourselfwich

This sandwich is often found at coffee shops, airports, or vending machines, and is composed of 80 percent bread with no condiments. It tastes slightly better than tree bark.

The Phug Yeahwich

Any sandwich with ingredients sloppily spilling out on all sides. Note that a sandwich can be any of the above and also a Phug Yeahwich.

SANDWICH PRINCIPLES

SANDWICH PRINCIPLE #1: The Bread-to-Stuff Ratio

The bread-to-stuff ratio is a make-or-break aspect of sandwiching. If you look at the profile of your sandwich and the bread thickness is greater than the stuff thickness, your sandwich has room for improvement. Aim to pack your sandwich with at least 50 percent stuff, but for a truly mind-blowing sandwich, target 75 to 600 percent stuff. Making an open-face sandwich is one way to ensure a strong bread-to-stuff ratio.

Think of the bread as the edible transport system that contains the meal. As my grandmother used to always think, "the less transport system, the better the sandwich."

When selecting your bread, consider its surface area, thickness, tensile strength, elasticity, and crumblature. A bread that is thin, wide, strong, one-half inch thick or less, with a tensile strength of 37MPa, elasticity of 6.3 units per stretchable inch, and a crumblature rating no higher than 4 is a strong choice.

SANDWICH PRINCIPLE #2: Moisture Content

The only thing worse than a dry sandwich is a really dry sandwich.

One of the key components in a sandwich with proper moisture content is fresh, moist bread. A bread that has the dampness of forest moss is ideal. This is easily accomplished by making a sandwich with two slices of fresh forest moss.

The next most important aspect of proper sandwich moisture levels is the sauces or condiments. As a general rule, start with an amount you think will taste good, then add more. But not so much more that it tastes bad. In other words, add the right amount, not the wrong amount. Always apply condiments to both slices of bread. Doing so will ensure that your bread doesn't dry out when exposed to air, which is the driest substance on Earth (aside from fire, sand, rocks, and balsa wood).

Another way to increase the moisture content of your sandwich is to add a slice of congealed water. If congealed water isn't available in your area, simply leave your sandwich out for half an hour when the morning dew materializes from Earth's nether region.

SANDWICH PRINCIPLE #3: Structure

The order of sandwich layers is very important for engineering structural integrity. You want to alternate between grippy/sticky and slippery layers. Your technique can include embedding condiments in the dead center of the sandwich if necessary, which can also aid in moisture distribution.

You can rate the structural integrity of your sandwich against the International Sandwich Structural Integrity Chart®. It is based on one's ability to hold the sandwich in various circumstances while eating it without any drops or drips.

INTERNATIONAL SANDWICH STRUCTURAL INTEGRITY CHART®

LEVEL 1: Holding the sandwich with two hands.

LEVEL 2: Holding the sandwich with two hands while walking.

LEVEL 3: One-handing the sandwich.

LEVEL 4: One-handing the sandwich on a pogo stick.

LEVEL 5: One-handing the sandwich while driving a motorcycle through a cornfield.

LEVEL 6: One-handing the sandwich while piloting a spaceship during takeoff.

LEVEL 7: One-handing a sandwich while riding a bull for 8 seconds.

LEVEL 8: One-handing a sandwich while riding a bull for 8 seconds while piloting a spaceship during take-off through a cornfield.

LEVEL 9: One-handing a sandwich while being picked up by an F5 tornado while riding a space bull.

LEVEL 10: One-handing a sandwich while traveling through a wormhole to the universe next door.

LEVEL 11: One-handing a sandwich while dying, then finishing it on the other side.

SANDWICH PRINCIPLE #4: Homogeny

Occasionally during your lifetime, you might have found that a sandwich has patches of blank bread. This sandwich is one that was made by a bad person. You, however, are not. Spread condiments on your bread from crust to crust, leaving no surface bread molecule untouched, then compliment yourself for doing a good job. Make sure your ingredients reach, at minimum, to the edge of the bread, if not flowing over the sides to a maximum distance of 8 inches. Make sure your compliments flow over your whole body and into your heart, where your emotions live within its protective walls.

☐ where ingredients should go.

■ where ingredients should also go.

SANDWICH PRINCIPLE #5: Pickles

The pickles principle is as follows: Always involve pickles in your sandwich. The benefits of adding pickles to your sandwich could be an entire book unto itself, but I will focus on the most important few:

A ➜ Pickles complete the flavor of your sandwich by adding the delicious taste of pickles.

B ➜ Adding pickles to your sandwich solves the common problem of not having pickles on your sandwich.

C ➜ A sandwich with pickles tastes far superior to a sandwich without pickles.

D ➜ A sandwich with pickles has a superior texture to a sandwich without pickles.

E ➜ Pickles are great.

F ➜ Pickles are the opposite of bad.

G ➜ Putting pickles on your sandwich makes you a good person.

There are certain people in this world who claim to not like pickles. They are in denial, as everybody loves pickles on account of the fact that pickles:

A ➜ Taste delicious, and

B ➜ Are wonderful.

For those who are convinced they do not like pickles, there are several ways to deal with this confounding issue:

1 → Learn to like pickles.

2 → Learn to don't not like pickles.

3 → Alter the gene within you that prevents you from thinking you don't dislike pickles.

4 → Investigate unconscious past life incidents that interfere with consciously liking pickles currently. If one is discovered, obtain a flux capacitor and the requisite amount of uranium to travel to the past to disrupt the incident that prevents you from liking pickles while not disrupting the space-time continuum.

5 → Dress your pickle up as another vegetable that you are quite fond of to trick your taste buds.

6 → Decide to live your best life. The life where you like pickles.

BREAKFAST
SANDWICHEST MEDIUMEST

I got into a huge fight with my editor over whether or not this sandwich belonged in the breakfast section, or the sandwich section. The fight played out while I was in the shower, alone, wrestling with this important categorization question, and fortunately I won. The truth is, a breakfast sandwich should be enjoyed at any meal, and at any speed—not just medium.

SERVES 1

2 strips bacon

2 eggs

2 slices bread

2 tablespoons mayo

¼ cup shredded cheddar cheese

2 to 4 tomato slices

Fine sea salt and freshly ground pepper

1 dill pickle, thinly sliced lengthwise

¼ avocado

Hot sauce

Ketchup (optional, see Note)

1 → Heat a medium skillet over medium heat, then add the bacon. Cook, flipping at your leisure, for 7 to 10 minutes, until the bacon is almost crisp and some fat has rendered. Remove the bacon from the pan and set aside.

2 → Crack the eggs into the greasy pan. Stir as they cook, using your wangjangler to corral them into the shape of your bread.

3 → Just before your eggs are cooked enough to flip, pop the bread into the toaster, then remove the pan from the heat and flip the eggs (see Note). When the bread has transformed into toast, spread the mayo on one side of each slice.

4 → Put the eggs on the mayo side of one slice, then sprinkle the cheddar on top. Add the bacon, sliced tomatoes, salt and pepper to taste, and dill pickle in that order. Mash the avocado onto the other mayo-slathered piece of toast, dab with hot sauce to your liking, and place it on top of the pickles to complete the sandwich. Eat it hot.

NOTES

The residual heat of your pan should be enough to finish the eggs once they're flipped, which is why I suggest taking them off the burner altogether. Just barely cooked eggs are divine. If you enjoy the texture of rubber, keep cooking the eggs on medium for several minutes longer. Alternatively, you can add a layer of fresh rubber to the sandwich.

A thin, almost imperceptible layer of ketchup, spread on top of the eggs, can add a sweet note that really brings the flavor home. Try it if you feel like something is missing. If you try it and you still feel like something is missing, it may be that you're lacking a significant other in your life, and once you find true love, the sandwich will taste much, much better, with or without ketchup. At least for the first few weeks. If the sandwich starts to taste like there's something missing again, you will have to look inside yourself instead.

TURKEY ROMAINE
SLAB

This breadless, carbless, nearly weightless open-face sandwich might make you question whether or not the word "sandwich" has any meaning at all. One thing to keep in mind with all open-face sandwiches is that the ingredients have zero aerial protection, which means this sort of sandwich is not ideal for eating in the pouring rain, or during an aggressive hailstorm. However, the waterproof underlayer makes this the best possible sandwich to eat while surfing, snorkeling, or stomping around in a dirty rain puddle.

SERVES 1

1 romaine lettuce leaf

1 tablespoon mayonnaise

2 slices smoked turkey, plus more as desired

¼ avocado, sliced

Fine sea salt and freshly ground pepper

1 teaspoon hot sauce, or to taste

1 → Admire the romaine leaf's perfectly inviting concave curvature. Spread the mayo on the romaine like you would on a slice of bread, but not *too* close to the edges. There is no crust to guide you here. I trust you, so trust yourself.

2 → Lay the 2 turkey slices on top (use more turkey if you prefer). Place the avocado slices down the center. Season with salt and pepper and dab with hot sauce. Take a bite, and think about pickles while you are chewing.

NOTES
Notice we are deliberately breaking the rules of homogeny here, as there is no need to slather the mayo up to the edge of the lettuce, or even evenly. That's because this sandwich gets folded into a half-pipe as it enters the mouth, resulting in a natural blending of the ingredients.

If you're making this slab for a friend, a fun trick to play is to dot the hot sauce into a specific shape, then see if your friend is smart enough to connect the dots. Will she notice that you've created a pointillist giraffe, or will she be too hungry to care? If your friend notices the shape and wants to connect the dots with more hot sauce to complete the picture, STOP HER IMMEDIATELY. If she uses a bunch more hot sauce to draw the giraffe, then the giraffe will be red, which is the wrong color for giraffes.

CURRY EGG SALAD

SANDWICH

Egg salad sandwiches are never to be eaten in enclosed public spaces, such as airplanes, buses, or dentist waiting rooms. It's considered inconsiderate to do so because if someone sees you eating an egg salad sandwich they might become jealous if they don't have one of their own. If you pick up on this jealous energy, you may feel distracted from enjoying your sandwich. In some instances, a person may attempt to sneak a bite of your sandwich, which could be dangerous if they bite your hand instead. Avoid this awkward and potentially violent situation by only eating egg salad sandwiches at home. Alone. At night. In the dark.

MAKES 2
CLOSED-FACE
SANDWICHES,
3 OPEN-FACE
SANDWICHES, OR
1 THICK CLOSED-FACE
SANDWICH WITH A
FEW BITES OF EGG
SALAD ON THE SIDE
WHILE YOU'RE MAKING
IT BECAUSE IT'S SO
GOOD YOU CAN'T HELP
YOURSELF AND NO
ONE NEEDS TO SEE
YOU HANGRY

3 large eggs

2 tablespoons mayonnaise

2 medium dill pickles, diced

½ teaspoon yellow
curry powder

Fine sea salt and freshly
ground pepper

2, 3, or 4 slices bread

1 ➜ Fill a medium saucepan with water and bring to a boil over high heat. Reduce the heat to medium, then gently lower the eggs into the water with a spoon, one at a time, and boil for 9 minutes. Remove the saucepan from the heat, drain off the water, then add cold water to cool the eggs.

2 ➜ Once the eggs are cool enough to handle, peel them. If the heat reemerges, run them under cold water for a few seconds and continue peeling. Roughly chop the peeled eggs and place them in a medium bowl. Add the mayo, pickles, curry powder, and salt and pepper to taste, then mash it all together using a fork.

3 ➜ Spread the egg salad on bread and eat open- or closed-face, but avoid eating two-faced.

NOTES
Be mindful of how much the boiling water throws the eggs around, as too much exuberance can cause them to crack. Adjust the heat to create a gentle boil.

You might be tempted to peel the eggs over the garbage can. This method is what's known in the food industry as "disgusting." Use two bowls: one for the eggs, the other for the shells. Compost the egg shells, or dye them various colors and glue them to blue construction paper, then give it as a gift to someone you don't like very much.

TUNA SALAD
SANDWICH

This moment, right now, may be the first time you've considered making a tuna sandwich without mayonnaise. If so, you may need therapy to cope with Residual Mayonnaise Withdrawal Syndrome. You may need therapy for all kinds of other issues as well, and overcoming a mayonnaise block is a great introductory subject to get you into a therapist's office while you build up the courage to discuss the meaty stuff, such as your aversion to gravy.

SERVES 2

1 (5-ounce) can solid white albacore tuna in water, drained

2 tablespoons olive oil

1 tablespoon balsamic vinegar

2 scallions, finely chopped

⅓ cup dried cherries (or dried fruit of your choice), chopped

¼ teaspoon fine sea salt

Freshly ground pepper

4 slices bread or 2 slices toast

2 gherkins or cornichons

1 → Add the tuna to a medium bowl and use a fork to break it apart into small pieces. Add the olive oil, balsamic vinegar, scallions, dried cherries, salt, and pepper to taste and recklessly mash them all together until they are mixed thoroughly.

2 → Sandwich the tuna between 2 slices bread to make 2 closed-face sandwiches, or top 2 pieces toast for open-face sandwiches. Now eat it with gherkins on the side. Also admire how I used "sandwich" as both a verb and a noun in the same sentence.

NOTES

The reason the open-face version of this sandwich is best with toast, as opposed to bread, is because open-face tuna on bread is a structural integrity disaster waiting to happen. The reason the closed-face version of this sandwich is best with bread, as opposed to toast, is that 2 slices of toast will result in a sandwich that's a bit too dry. Although you could get away with a very light toasting. Sandwichcraft is a game that should be played to win.

LEEKY BACON POCKET

This sandwich was originally a side dish. Bacon and leeks just sounded good together. But then I needed another sandwich, so I thought: Bacon and leeks sound good, and so does bread and tzatziki. Which is cheating because tzatziki sounds great on everything. I might have been better off making a burger instead. But it's too late now.

Also, this recipe contains red wine vinegar. If you're a baby, remember that drinking wine is against the law for you. Also remember that you are too young to know how to read, unless you're so young that you haven't learned that you can't read yet, in which case make sure you're not drinking any form of wine.

SERVES 2

4 strips bacon, chopped
into 1-inch pieces

2 cups sliced leeks (from
1 large leek excluding
the last 2 inches of green;
see Notes on page 110)

1 tablespoon olive oil

1 teaspoon red wine vinegar

2 9-inch pitas, halved
crosswise

2 tablespoons tzatziki or
Greek yogurt

1 ➜ Heat a large skillet over medium heat and add the bacon. Cook about 4 minutes, or until the bacon fat covers the bottom of the pan. Add the leeks and wangjangle until the leeks are coated in bacon fat. Add the olive oil and red wine vinegar and wangjangle again.

2 ➜ Reduce the heat to medium-low and simmer for about 10 minutes, or until the bacon is cooked through but not quite crispy and the leeks are soft.

3 ➜ Open the pita and spread tzatziki on both inner sides. Fill each pita with bacony leeks. Eat while listening to the sound of pickles.

NOTES
You can make two pitas, or one bigger pita. I personally make one bigger pita but my friend Allison once made this recipe and insisted that it made two pitas-worth of stuff. I trust her, but then again I don't know how hungry she is on a regular basis. Or on an irregular basis.

Another option is to stuff one pita as much as possible, and then share it, achieving a higher ratio of stuff to bread, which is good. You could also pass each half back and forth, taking turns with each bite, and pretend you're living in a time before we were aware of germs.

(RECIPE CONTINUES)

NOTES ON LEEKS

It's difficult to express just how much dirt there is in leeks. One way would be to say "Man, there's a whole lot of dirt in leeks." Another way might be "SERIOUSLY? That's a lot of damn dirt!" Another way might be "I expected that. I've cooked with leeks before."

Recent USDA guidelines state that leeks may contain no more than 85% dirt. Part of the reason there is so much dirt in leeks is because they grow out of the ground, where a large percentage of the Earth's dirt is stored.

The easiest way to clean a leek is to hold it up in front of a fire hose on full blast. The easiest way to make that happen is to set your house on fire, then hold the leek up in an open window, and hope the fire department responds swiftly.

If you don't have a fire department in your area, the next best way to clean a leek is to cut it in half lengthwise, hold one of the dirty-ended halves under the tap, then rifle through the layers like a deck of cards. Unless you ask my really good friend Amanda, who thinks the best way to clean a leek is to slice them and soak them, then lift them out of the water. I bet she's never even tried the card-rifling trick. And I bet she'd make a terrible magician.

The easiest way to tell if a layer of your leek has dirt is this: If you see a layer, and that layer is part of a leek, then it has dirt. If you buy a leek that doesn't have dirt in the layers, then you've basically won the lottery. It's the saddest lottery on Earth, but yay, you won.

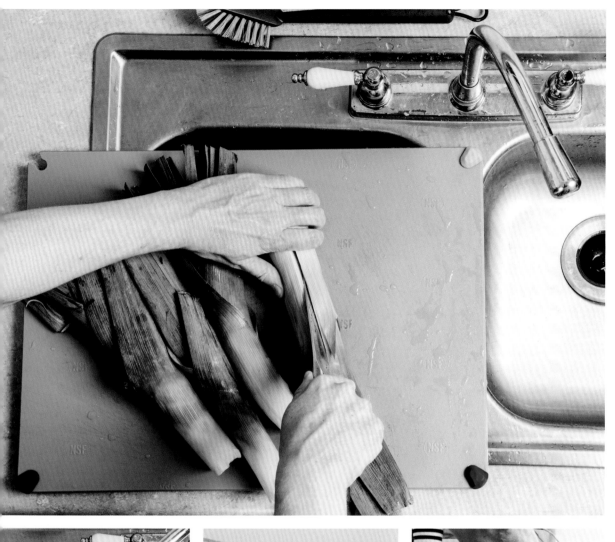

HAM AND CHEESE
MELT

Some people are very passionate about the names they give their sandwiches. While I called this sandwich a Ham and Cheese Melt, some might call it a Grilled Cheese with Ham and Pickles. But they might find themselves on the business end of an earful about sandwich names. You see, there are Grilled Cheese Purists out there who insist that a grilled cheese must consist of nothing more than bread, butter, and cheese. As soon as you add more ingredients, they say, the sandwich is no longer a grilled cheese—it becomes a melt.

On the other hand, others insist that as long as it is a cheesy sandwich fried in a pan, it remains a grilled cheese. It's simply an enhanced grilled cheese. If I add a spoiler to my station wagon, they argue, does it cease to be a station wagon? If I put clothes on my baby, they say, does it cease to be a baby? What if that baby grows into a teenager, is it still not a baby?

It's best not to get involved in these arguments. Instead, before serving a grilled cheese or melt, ask everyone in the room what they prefer to call it. Anyone who cares what it's called doesn't get a sandwich.

SERVES 1

1 tablespoon salted butter, softened

2 slices bread

1 cup shredded cheddar cheese

2 slices smoked ham

1 medium dill pickle, thinly sliced lengthwise

2 teaspoons honey mustard

1 → Preheat a medium skillet over medium heat. Butter each slice of bread on one side and place one slice butter side down in the pan, then sprinkle on half the cheddar. Lay the ham on top of that, then sprinkle the rest of the cheese on top of that.

2 → Add the second piece of bread, butter side up, cover, and cook for 2 to 3 minutes, until the bottom slice is golden brown, then flip the sandwich, replace the cover, and cook for 1 to 2 minutes more, until the second side is golden brown.

3 → Remove the sandwich from the pan, slide a fork between the 2 slices of ham, and lift up the top. Add a layer of dill pickles, spread honey mustard on the top side, then put the sandwich back together.

4 → Cut the sandwich in half and eat it using the hole that's in your face. The one above your chin. Not the ones above your mouth.

NOTES

Did you know that some people spread mayonnaise on the outside of the bread when pan-frying a sandwich instead of butter? Resist the impulse to judge, consider that they might know something you don't, and then allow the disdainful feelings to wash over you like a haughty baptismal ceremony.

The mayonnaise adds a tangy flavor and produces beautiful golden crustitude. That's on account of the ingredient "tang" that is in all mayonnaises. Using butter adds a buttery flavor. That's because of the butter. Maybe you should give the mayonnaise a try. Or maybe you'd prefer to never evolve and spend the rest of your life barely living in your small, small world.

SWEET TOMATO
GRILLED
CHEESE PITA

With this sandwich, not only have I broken the Grilled Cheese Purist rules, but I have also gone ahead and used a nontraditional grilled cheese bread. This is practically a wrap with hot tomato jam. I am almost asking to be physically attacked at this point.

Which I would welcome.

Since I have a yellow belt in taekwondo, I am nearly indestructible. Not physically though. Physically I am very weak. I can easily throw my shoulder out from tossing a baseball. I never really got the hang of it. I think it was a confidence issue I had as a kid, which carried over into an overconfidence issue I have as an adult. But on a spirit level, I am quite strong. And that's because of the yellow belt.

SERVES 2

1 tablespoon olive oil

2 garlic cloves, finely chopped or pressed

1½ cups chopped, seeded tomatoes (about 2 medium)

1 teaspoon maple syrup

Fine sea salt and freshly ground pepper

1 9-inch pita, halved crosswise

1½ cups shredded cheddar cheese

1 teaspoon salted butter

1 → In a medium nonstick skillet, heat the oil over medium heat until it shimmers like the thighs of the oiled-up Greek wrestler you're about to grapple with. Add the garlic and tomatoes, stir to coat them in oil, and cook for 2 minutes, until soft.

2 → Reduce the heat to medium-low and add the maple syrup and a pinch each of salt and pepper. Cook for about 20 minutes, wangjangling occasionally, until the tomatoes reduce into a thick, jammy sauce.

3 → Open up half of the pita horizontally to make a pocket, and sprinkle in one-quarter of the cheese. Spoon in half the tomato jam, then add another one-quarter of the cheese on top. Repeat with the other pita half.

4 → In a separate nonstick medium skillet, or clean the one you just used, melt the butter on medium heat. Cook the pita for 2 minutes on each side, until the cheese is melted and the bread is toasty and golden.

5 → With every bite, inhale deeply while imagining the fragrance of pickles.

SOUPS AND SALADS

Soups and salads are natural enemies. Soups are composed of 90% scalding water, while salads are composed of 90% cold air. Grouping them together on menus and in cookbooks was originally done to try to coax the foods into getting along, but it has never been successful.

Eventually, chefs realized that something more important was taking place. The animosity created by grouping natural enemies together produces Meal Tension, which can only be resolved by the serving of the main dish. This phenomenon allows chefs to create cheap, subpar main dishes that taste way better than they otherwise would because of the emotional relief you feel once the food enemies are safely digesting in your stomach.

Chefs hate me for exposing this secret, because it means they have to start focusing on creating mains that taste delicious, rather than relying on cheap, manipulative, gimmicks. When you're eating at a restaurant, be aware and be safe. Don't fall for their tricks.

By the way, to estimate how much dressing to make for a specific quantity of salad, simply make the amount of dressing you would put on one lettuce leaf, then count the number of lettuce leaves you want to dress, and multiply the dressing amount by the leaf number to get your total dressing quantity.

EASIEST
SALAD
DRESSING
ON EARTH

First of all, the title of this recipe is a lie. There are easier salad dressings with even fewer ingredients. But this is the easiest salad dressing on Earth that has the fullest flavor that I know of. And I don't know much.

Keep in mind that vinaigrettes are emulsions, which means they are emulsified, which means that once they're combined they will separate again. So regardless of when you've wang-jangled it together, always give it one last wangjangulation just before pouring it on your salad. If you're making this recipe around other people, say things out loud such as "Emulsions, amiright?" or "Emulsions are a lot of work, but I wouldn't have it any other way."

MAKES ¼ CUP

3 tablespoons olive oil

1 tablespoon balsamic vinegar

1 teaspoon Dijon mustard

Pinch of fine sea salt

Freshly ground pepper

1 ➡ In a small bowl, measuring cup, container, or mug, combine the olive oil, balsamic vinegar, mustard, and salt and pepper to taste, and wangjangle vigorously until combined, or shake inside a sealed mason jar.

2 ➡ If you want to make a larger quantity to use regularly, store it in the fridge in a sealed container for up to 2 weeks. Rewangjangle and allow it to come up to room temperature before using.

NOTES

This dressing is very forgiving and can be easily eyeballed with a wide spectrum of ratios that will still taste good, even if you royally mess it up, so don't sweat it because it's nearly unmessupable. If you do somehow manage to royally mess it up, just tell yourself that it will be okay, even though it won't. That's the power of affirmation in action.

To make it without measuring, start by pouring some olive oil into the mixing vessel of your choice. Eyeball what one-third of the olive oil looks like, then add that amount of vinegar. Eyeball what half of the vinegar looks like, then add that amount of mustard. Add a pinch of salt and some pepper, wangjangle, and adjust to your liking. You're allowed to feel a little bit proud.

If it tastes like you have too much balsamic vinegar, add in a little more mustard. If it tastes too much like mustard, add in a touch more balsamic. If it tastes too strong, add in a little more olive oil. Continue compensating until you have several barrels full of the easiest salad dressing on Earth.

SECOND EASIEST
SALAD
DRESSING
ON EARTH

This recipe title is also a lie, but for the sake of coherence, let's just roll with it. You might think that this dressing would taste remarkably similar to the first dressing, since only one ingredient is added, but you are wrong.

The magic of sesame oil is that it pretty much hijacks your taste buds and forces you to focus on it. But you'll still taste everything else if you look for it. But don't look with your eyes. Look with your mouth. And don't look too hard. Just enjoy that sesame.

MAKES ⅓ CUP

3 tablespoons olive oil

1 tablespoon balsamic vinegar

1 teaspoon Dijon mustard

1 teaspoon sesame oil

Pinch of fine sea salt

Freshly ground pepper

1 ➜ In a small bowl, measuring cup, container, jar, or mug, combine the olive oil, balsamic vinegar, Dijon mustard, sesame oil, and salt and pepper to taste, and wangjangle vigorously until combined. You can also shake if there's a lid.

2 ➜ If you want to make a larger quantity to use regularly, store it in the fridge in a sealed container for up to 2 weeks. Rewangjangle and allow it to come up to room temperature before using.

THIRD EASIEST
SALAD
DRESSING
ON EARTH

I'm not going to comment on the accuracy of the recipe title here. We've already established a pattern of lies and there's no need to further highlight the problem. Let's just quietly move forward with the understanding that not everyone is perfect no matter how hard he tries to write a good title for a salad dressing recipe. I'd like to see *you* write one. Actually, I would not like to see that, because it will probably be a good title and that will just exacerbate the problem I'm having and I really don't need that right now.

This version of the recipe adds a creaminess that's difficult to describe. I guess the best word to use would be "creamishness." The avocado calms and blends the flavors, makes it thicker, and adds a flavor that's unique to the avocado. Avocado flavor.

MAKES ¾ CUP

3 tablespoons olive oil

1 tablespoon balsamic vinegar

1 teaspoon Dijon mustard

1 teaspoon sesame oil

Pinch of fine sea salt

Freshly ground pepper

1 small avocado, mashed

1 → In a small bowl, measuring cup, container, jar, or mug, combine the olive oil, balsamic vinegar, Dijon mustard, sesame oil, salt, and pepper to taste and wangjangle vigorously until blended thoroughly.

2 → Mash in the avocado to create a vinaigrette with creamishness. It takes more effort to mix this dressing into greens, but it tastes excellent with a fantastic texture so don't be lazy. Be awesome.

3 → If you'd like to make a larger quantity of this dressing to store and use later, I'm sorry but I don't recommend it. The avocado just isn't going to keep like the rest of the ingredients so I suggest making it on a case-by-case basis when your avocado is nice and ripe, and you're in the mood to put a little elbow grease into your salad dressing, in addition to that olive grease.

BASIC BORING
MIXED GREEN SALAD

Developing the urge to eat salad is a skill. It requires training and discipline, but once you get over the hump, the cravings take over and eating salad becomes easy.

The reason it is difficult at first is because of the high quantity of air that's in salad. The body is accustomed to breathing, rather than eating, air, so it takes some training to convince the body that it's okay to eat a bowl of mostly nothing. But once your body stops being afraid, that's when the real magic begins. Salad magic.

The magic starts here.

SERVES 4

7 cups mixed greens

1 cup sliced cherry or grape tomatoes

1 cup sliced cucumber (1 small)

⅓ cup salted roasted sunflower seeds

Second Easiest Salad Dressing on Earth (page 120)

In a large bowl, combine the greens, tomatoes, cucumber, and sunflower seeds. Pour the dressing on top, then wangjangle until mixed thoroughly. Serve cold or piping hot.*

NOTE

* I highly recommend that you do not serve this salad piping hot. I only said that to give you the illusion of choice, assuming you would make the correct one. But I'm adding this note now because I don't trust you.

CREAMY RAW
BROCCOLI
SALAD

This salad is what's known as a "sleeper salad." Most people, when surveying the buffet table, will turn their nose up as they walk by. Some might say "Wet broccoli? No thanks." Others might say "Green broccoli? You've got to be kidding me." But the ones who taste it will be in on the secret of its deliciousness, and might just insult it out loud in order to keep others away.

The other reason creamy raw broccoli salad is known as a sleeper salad is because broccoli is never harvested when it is awake.

SERVES 4

½ **cup mayonnaise**

½ **cup sour cream**

2 **teaspoons sesame oil**

½ **teaspoon fine sea salt**

4 **cups roughly chopped broccoli (from 2 medium heads)**

Juice of ½ **lime**

Freshly ground pepper

1 ➡ In a small bowl, combine the mayo, sour cream, sesame oil, and salt and wangjangle thoroughly.

2 ➡ In a large bowl, combine the broccoli and dressing and wangjangle to coat evenly. Add the lime juice and give a final stir. Finish the sleeper salad with pepper to taste and serve chilled or at room temperature.

NOTES

See page 188 for a surprise, treasure-hunt-style tip. Except that now that I've told you, it won't be a surprise at all. But now that you're expecting it to not be a surprise, you might end up being surprised. And now that I've built up the surprise (or nonsurprise, depending how you look at it), your expectations will certainly make sure that even if you're surprised, you'll definitely be disappointed. And maybe the disappointment is actually the surprise. That's what happens when you make a big deal about something that isn't a big deal at all. Or am I playing it down in order to lower your expectations so that you will, in fact, be surprised, just like I mentioned at the beginning? I'm not even sure at this point. Or am I absolutely certain, and I just said that so I wouldn't have to take responsibility for your reaction? I could easily tell you the tip right here in this paragraph. Perhaps it's in the very next sentence, and not on page 188. Except that it's not. Surprise! You're going to have to use those lazy fingers of yours and go tip hunting, which you might think is less dangerous than actual hunting, which shows how little you know about the human mind, the most dangerous place of all.

QUINOA SALAD

A quinoa salad like this is often referred to as a summer salad. The reason it's considered a summer salad is because it won't get disgusting after sitting for an hour in your beach bag. Hopefully, I mean. Don't hold me to that. I don't like the beach, I'm afraid of bags, and I don't believe in the sun.

The other reason it's called a summer salad is because unlike lettuce, quinoa doesn't grow in the winter.

SERVES 4 TO 6

1 cup quinoa

1 teaspoon fine sea salt

FOR THE DRESSING

¼ cup olive oil

2 tablespoons red wine vinegar

2 shallots, diced

½ teaspoon maple syrup or honey

FOR THE SALAD

1 (15.5-ounce) can chickpeas, drained and rinsed

1 cup Kalamata olives, pitted and roughly chopped

Juice of ½ lemon

Freshly ground pepper

1 ➜ In a medium saucepan, combine the quinoa, salt, and 2 cups water. Bring to a boil over high heat, then reduce the heat to low, cover, and simmer for about 12 minutes, or until the liquid has completely evaporated. Remove the pan from the heat and fluff the quinoa with a fork.

2 ➜ Meanwhile, make the dressing: In a small bowl, combine the olive oil, red wine vinegar, shallots, and maple syrup or honey, whisk vigorously, and allow them to sit and get to know each other. Feel free to mash the shallots against the inside of your vessel with a fork to squeeze out additional shallot juice.

3 ➜ Assemble the salad: In a large bowl, combine the quinoa, chickpeas, and olives. Whisk the dressing again just before adding it to the quinoa. Toss to combine. Add the lemon juice, season the salad with pepper to taste, and give it another toss. Serve immediately or after cooling in the fridge. Or on flimsy paper plates at the beach on a day full of powerful, unexpected gusts of wind.

NOTE
If you've never cooked with shallots before, welcome to a wonderful new chapter of your life. They have an awesome, mild, oniony flavor. You may be thinking: How can I get shallots as big as onions? But the sad truth is, you can't. Shallots are destined to be enjoyed in small, delicious, mind-blowing micro-doses.

BROCCOLI CHEDDAR SOUP

People don't usually think about drinking broccoli or cheese. But if you make this soup, that's what you'll be doing. I know we always say eating soup rather than drinking soup, but that's not the truth. You're drinking it, not chewing it, unless it's a chunky soup, which this is not. It's less appealing to think of it this way. That's why we don't say it. But at some point the lies need to stop. And that point is right here. Literally, the period of the previous sentence. That's when we changed the world.

SERVES 4

4 cups veggie broth

6 cups roughly chopped broccoli (from 2 medium heads)

2 cups shredded cheddar cheese

Freshly ground pepper

1 ➔ In a medium saucepan, bring the broth to a boil over high heat. Add the broccoli, then reduce the heat to medium-low, simmering gently for 25 minutes, until softened.

2 ➔ Remove the saucepan from the heat, allow to cool for 10 minutes, and then use an immersion blender to puree. Or simply mash it with a hand masher if you don't want to bother with blending at all; it's still good. If you use the hand masher, make sure to wear a tank top to show off your impressive muscle definition. (You can also see my note with the following recipe about using a regular blender—carefully.)

3 ➔ Add the shredded cheddar and stir until it's melted and well combined. Add pepper to taste. Divide the soup among bowls and serve.

4 ➔ Good luck cleaning the cheese off the pot LOL OMG you'll never make this again. No seriously, move the soup to bowls and clean the pot while it's still hot. Cleaning a dried cheese pot is actual hell. In fact, you'll wish you were actually in hell instead of cleaning that cheese off the pot.

5 ➔ Also, hell doesn't actually exist. It's not a real thing. So don't worry about suffering for all of eternity in the afterlife. I've been to the other side a few times and I promise you that will never happen.

NOTE
Vegetable broths have a wide range of saltiness. If you make your broth with bouillon cubes, you might want to make it at half strength, then adjust the salt or bouillon upward from there, especially since the cheese is also salty. If you can't figure it out, just give me a call and I'll talk you through it.

LIZZY'S CAULIFLOWER SOUP

I learned this recipe from my friend Lizzy. I changed her name here to avoid potential legal action (her name is actually Louise). She's been trying to sue me for years, but I won't give her the opportunity, nor the honor. Instead I will profit off of her good ideas, and eventually disappear without a trace. This is the natural Friendship Cycle in the modern world.

Don't get me wrong, we have an excellent friendship full of love, sharing, trust, and openness. I'm just pretty sure this conflict is what's brewing under the surface. I ripped out these pages in the copy of the book I gave to her. That's why the numbers on these pages are the same as the numbers on the previous pages. She'll never figure it out.

Lizzy is also the person who told me about how good things taste when you cook them until they are brown. While I now know it's called the Maillard reaction, I don't think she knew that when she told me (see page 39). But she had a baby recently so she probably knows more about what it takes to raise a kid than I do. But I could probably give her a few hot parenting tips that would really help her out.

By the way, hot parenting tips are best given to parents by nonparents when the parents are feeling frustrated and had a bad night's sleep. That's the best time to show them how they're doing things wrong. The tips are best prefaced with "Well, if I had a kid . . ." Your parent friends will be very appreciative of your insight.

SERVES 4

4 cups cauliflower florets (from 1 large head)

1 large yellow onion, diced

3 garlic cloves, peeled but whole

3 tablespoons olive oil

3½ cups chicken or veggie broth

Fine sea salt and freshly ground pepper

1 ➔ Preheat the oven to 400°F. Line a baking sheet with parchment paper.

2 ➔ In a large bowl, combine the cauliflower, three-quarters of the onion, the garlic cloves, and 2 tablespoons of the olive oil and wangjangle until coated. Arrange the veggies on the prepared baking sheet and roast for 25 to 30 minutes, until they start to brown.

3 ➔ In a large saucepan, bring the broth to a boil over high heat, then add the roasted veggies. Reduce the heat to low, cover, and simmer for 10 to 15 minutes, until the veggies are very soft.

LOUISE

4 → Remove the saucepan from the heat, allow to cool for 10 minutes, then puree with an immersion blender while being very careful of the steam and splashing. Keep the immersion blender submerged and do not lift it out of the soup while it's still running. If necessary, use a knife to cut down the larger chunks inside the pot to make them a more immersion-blender-friendly size. Add salt and pepper to taste.

5 → In a medium skillet, heat the remaining 1 tablespoon olive oil over medium-high heat until it shimmers like your heart at the thought of a room full of puppies. Add the remaining onion and sauté for 7 to 10 minutes, until it's beyond golden and well into burnt territory (see Maillard overreaction, page 39).

6 → Divide the soup among bowls and serve with a spoonful of the overly toasty onion garnish on top.

NOTES

If you don't have an immersion blender, you can use a regular blender to puree the soup, but you must obey these important safety tips to avoid having the soup explode out the top (and that's no joke): Allow the soup to cool for 15 minutes so that there's less steam. Do not fill your blender more than halfway. Remove the blender top center insert and cover with a folded towel to allow steam to escape. Start the blender on slow and bring it up to speed. If your blender only operates with a completely sealed top, do not use it to blend hot liquids.

When serving this dish to a good friend, tell them you've made a bowl of applesauce with a handful of dirt thrown on top. When they take a bite, yell, "Surprise it's actually soup!"*

*The lawyers at Clarkson Potter have made it abundantly clear that I must inform you that you should let your friend know that the applesauce is very hot and to be extra careful when eating it. And also that you should usually avoid more than 2 tablespoons of dirt in any given dish.**

**The lawyers at Clarkson Potter have made it abundantly clear that I cannot recommend that you eat any dirt at all. Please don't eat dirt. Thank you.

POTATO SALAD

FOR THE LIVING

This is not the kind of potato salad you want to bring to a funeral. A funeral is about paying respect to the dead. And this potato salad would be a disrespectful gesture because it would pull all of the attention away from the person who died and place it on the potato salad instead. You could try to sneak it in, play it down, disguise it as a mediocre potato salad, but don't. It's not worth the risk. Everyone will be upset about how good it tastes and about how the person you were supposed to be celebrating couldn't possibly live up to how good it looks. So save this one for a potluck, OK?

SERVES 6

1 tablespoon fine sea salt

1½ pounds mini potatoes, halved or quartered

FOR THE DRESSING

4 scallions, finely chopped

3 tablespoons olive oil

1 tablespoon red wine vinegar

1 tablespoon whole-grain mustard

1 teaspoon honey

FOR THE SALAD

4 medium dill pickles, diced

¾ cup chopped or sliced salami or sausage

1 ➜ In a large saucepan, add the salt, the potatoes, and enough water to cover them by 2 inches. Bring to a boil over high heat, then reduce the heat to medium and simmer for about 10 minutes, until fork-tender. Drain the potatoes and transfer them to a large bowl.

2 ➜ Meanwhile, make the dressing: In a small bowl, measuring cup, container, or mug, combine the scallions, olive oil, red wine vinegar, whole-grain mustard, and honey and wangjangle.

3 ➜ Assemble the salad: Give the dressing a final wangjangling before you pour it onto the potatoes (or if you prefer, wongjongling works well for this dressing). Add the pickles and salami, and mix until well combined. Serve with the residual warmness of the potatoes or allow the salad to cool in the fridge first. It's good either way.

NOTES

When boiling potatoes, you have to trust the fork. The fork is the ultimate determiner of doneness, and once it slides through easily, the potatoes are done. Also, the potatoes will continue cooking from the residual heat once removed from the water, so "almost done" is often "done."

Allowing the scallions to soak in the dressing helps the scallion-y flavor to pervade the dressing. You can also mash the scallions against the side of your dressing vessel with a fork to really increase the scallionness of the dressing. Don't confuse dressing scallionness with The Dressing Scalioness, the most powerful and fierce scallion in all of Dressingland.

For a vegetarian version, simply pick out the bits of salami once the potato salad has cooled.

SPICY PEANUT BUTTER SOUP

If you were ever a kid, you might have spent some time eating peanut butter sandwiches. You might subconsciously think that the only place to put peanut butter is on a slice of bread, or perhaps a cracker, or combined with chocolate. The idea of hot peanut butter might make your whole body tense up, or at the very least make you cross your arms with reflexive skepticism. You'll be tempted to dismiss this soup as something that just won't work. So you won't make it. This is the reason I recommend never being a kid.

The bones of this soup were first introduced to me by my friend Emma. Much like The Bean Dip Formerly Known as Gregg's (page 76), I corrected her cooking mistakes to make this soup. And much like Lizzy (page 128), her name was changed here to avoid a potential lawsuit (it's actually Evalyn). But honestly, Emma couldn't sue her way out of a paper bag so I'm not too worried. Neither could Gregg, which is why I didn't even bother changing his name.

SERVES 6

2 tablespoons olive oil

1 large red onion, diced

4 cups veggie broth

4 cups roughly chopped broccoli (from 2 medium heads)

2 cups shredded carrots from two medium carrots

1 (28-ounce) can diced tomatoes, drained

1 (15.5-ounce) can chickpeas, drained and rinsed

¾ cup smooth peanut butter, preferably natural

2 to 3 teaspoons chili garlic sauce, to taste

1 teaspoon brown sugar

1 teaspoon fine sea salt

½ teaspoon freshly ground pepper

1 ➡ In a large saucepan, heat the olive oil over medium-high heat until it shimmers like sunbeams reflecting off the Queen's freshly polished teapot. Add the onion and sauté for 5 minutes, stirring frequently, until just beginning to brown. Add the broth, broccoli, carrots, tomatoes, chickpeas, peanut butter, chili garlic sauce, brown sugar, salt, and pepper. Wangjangle thoroughly.

2 ➡ Reduce the heat to medium-low, cover, and simmer for 30 minutes, or until everything is cooked through. Uncover and continue simmering, stirring occasionally, until your desired thickness is reached. The longer you simmer, the thicker it will get. Kind of like the opposite of whittling.

3 ➡ Divide the soup among bowls and serve hot. Don't share with Emma.

VEGGIES
ON THE SIDE

Side dishes are dishes that were traditionally eaten at the side of the house due to their shameful nature. These dishes usually consisted of oblong and phallus-shaped vegetables, shiny grains, and turnips. Shameful ingredients also included vegetables with no moral compass, such as pumpkins and beets.

For years, many people lived happily without eating side dishes, digging into potatoes and meat pies with a sense of righteousness. Side dish lovers were forced underground into dirty vegetable speakeasies, where patrons could indulge their love of forbidden produce while also enjoying moving picture films portraying vegetable outcast love stories.

After several years, the stigma against these vegetables slowly eased off to the point where people were once again allowed to eat them on the sides of their houses. During a particularly angry winter, many people started eating them in their basements, then on the stairs, then on the floor below the table. Eventually they made it to the side of the plate, but we still don't have the courage to put these vegetables in the center. And hopefully we never will.

When choosing a side dish, it's important to ascertain whether or not the flavor of the side dish will contrast nicely with the main dish. You want something comple-mentary but different enough to create variety. If you're serving a risotto sandwich for your main, mashed potatoes on rice might make the meal taste overly starchy. However, if you're having frozen, raw ground beef for the main, the heat of the potatoes, along with the lack of dangerous bacteria, would contrast perfectly.

The other main aspect of choosing side dishes is how the personality of the ingredients will fit into the meal. Will the smugness of kale pair well with the standoffishness of Cornish hen? Will the unflappable optimism of radishes feel inappropriate when served with the somber vibe of stew? The answer is yes.

If making a side dish to pair with your main feels like way too much of a hassle, you can always serve your main with a side of steamed multivitamins.

ROASTED ASPARAGUS

WITH SLICED ALMONDS

Asparagus is known for its peaceful disposition, despite being Nature's Dagger. Heirloom asparagus is almost as tough as steel and it has taken generations of genetic engineering to finally get rid of the metallic taste.

Asparagus is also one of the fastest growing vegetables, shooting up from the ground in spurts, which, in rare cases, can result in stabbed feet. That's one of the reasons it's important to build a small fence around planted asparagus. The other reason is that most asparagi are criminals.

Someone once told me that the rules of high-end food etiquette state that asparagus is the only vegetable you are allowed to eat with your hands. I'm not sure whether this gives asparagus a sense of superiority, or if it feels singled out and would rather be like its more forkable pals. I'm also not sure whether this person was lying to me in an attempt to make me look like a fool at a black tie event she invited me to. Joke's on her. I eat everything with a pair of pliers.

SERVES 4

1 (12-ounce) bunch asparagus, trimmed

1½ tablespoons olive oil

2 tablespoons sliced almonds

1 teaspoon smoked paprika

½ teaspoon fine sea salt

1 → Preheat the oven to 400°F. Line a baking sheet with parchment paper.

2 → Arrange the asparagus on the baking sheet, drizzle with the olive oil, then evenly sprinkle the almonds, paprika, and salt on top. Roll the asparagus over each other until everything is coated evenly and the asparagi are lying parallel and are in a good mood.

3 → Roast the asparagus for about 15 minutes, until the almonds start to brown, watching them closely. If the almonds start getting really dark, remove the baking sheet from the oven. Transfer the asparagus to a platter and serve warm or at room temperature. Leave no almond slices behind—sprinkle any stragglers back on top.

ROASTED
MUSTARD
STRING
BEANS

String beans did not get their name because they contain string. That's a myth. String beans were named because they are known for stringing along other beans who are interested in them. Since all string beans look unremarkably similar, they have a hard time deciding who they are attracted to. This leads to a lot of hemming and hawing in addition to indecisiveness, ambivalence, wavering, and tentative vacillation. It's a miracle that string beans ever end up mating, but we know that they do because they keep showing up at the grocery store.

SERVES 4

14 ounces (about 3 cups) green beans, ends trimmed

1 tablespoon olive oil

2 teaspoons whole-grain Dijon mustard

1 teaspoon red wine vinegar

½ teaspoon fine sea salt

Freshly ground pepper

1 ➜ Preheat the oven to 400°F. Line a baking sheet with parchment paper.

2 ➜ In a large bowl, combine the green beans, olive oil, mustard, red wine vinegar, salt, and pepper to taste and wangjangle thoroughly. Arrange evenly on the prepared baking sheet and roast for 25 to 30 minutes, wrassling them once around halfway through, until they start to brown.

3 ➜ Allow to cool for 10 minutes before serving.

BRUSSAMIC SPROUTS

Brussels sprouts might be the vegetable that has had to deal with the most negative sentiment in vegetable history. Growing up, you might have thought that Brussels sprouts were literally garbage by the way they were portrayed by the media. You didn't need to try them to know they were repulsive, but you still wondered how people could be so negative about a vegetable.

And then one day you smelled the odor of wet garbage permeating the kitchen, as the soggy, flappy, cabbage-y, fleshy Brussels sprouts were leached of their flavor in boiling water and served tasting like hot earlobe slices. And you realized that everyone had actually been going easy on Brussels sprouts back in the day. And maybe it wasn't a coincidence that their initials are BS.

And this is why we love the Kitchen Hot Box. Boiling has its place, to be sure, but that place isn't Brussels sprouts. It's potatoes. Rice. Sterilizing needles. Use this recipe to counteract any residual negative feelings you might have toward Brussels sprouts from childhood brainwashing.

SERVES 4

3 cups (11 ounces) halved Brussels sprouts

2 tablespoons balsamic vinegar

1 tablespoon olive oil

½ teaspoon fine sea salt

2 tablespoons grated parmesan cheese

1 ➜ Preheat the oven to 400°F. Line a baking sheet with parchment paper.

2 ➜ In a large bowl, combine the Brussels sprouts and balsamic vinegar and wangjangle until the vinegar is thoroughly combined and has made its way into the dark fleshy folds of the BS. Add the olive oil and salt and rewangjangle until the Brussels sprouts are evenly coated.

3 ➜ Arrange the Brussels sprouts cut side down on the prepared pan. Roast for 30 minutes, or until the bottoms are browned.

4 ➜ Remove the Brussels sprouts from the oven, sprinkle with the parmesan, and allow them to cool for 10 minutes before serving.

NOTE
There are a number of differences to keep in mind when using big BS or small BS. Big BS are larger in size, for one. And the thickness of larger BS means that more time is required to cook through compared to smaller BS. If you have BS in a range of sizes, consider halving the biggest ones but don't halve the smallest ones so that they are around the same size when cooked. We are looking for consistent BS.

PAN-FRIED KALE

We need to talk about kale's hygiene. When washing kale, it's best to pretend that you're washing the hair of a wealthy prince in a high-end kale-washing salon. This will make sure you take care to be thorough, washing all of the nooks and crannies, and treating the kale with an abundance of care.

You're not treating the hair of the prince with extra care because the prince is wealthy and therefore deserves to have his hair treated better than anyone else. You're doing it because the prince has very strong bodyguards who will kick your ass if you don't do it right.

SERVES 4

2 tablespoons olive oil

4 garlic cloves, chopped
(2 tablespoons)

2 tablespoons chopped,
oil-packed sun-dried tomatoes

4 cups chopped kale,
stems removed

½ teaspoon fine sea salt,
plus more to taste

Freshly ground pepper

Juice of ¼ lemon

1 → In a large nonstick skillet, heat the oil over medium heat until it shimmers like a flock of happy golden butterflies. Add the garlic and sun-dried tomatoes, and cook for 1 minute, until fragrant.

2 → Add the kale, spreading it around to coat it in oil. Once the kale starts to shrink, add the salt and pepper to taste. Continue cooking for about 3 minutes, stirring occasionally, until the kale is around one-quarter of its original volume.

3 → Squeeze the lemon juice over top. Taste and adjust the salt and pepper if needed, and go ahead and add more lemon if you prefer. Serve.

NOTE
The lemon juice is especially important in this dish because it balances out the bitterness of the kale. The bitterness of the kale is due to its smug and condescending nature. Attempts to breed the smugness out of kale resulted in kale that was so happy it was nauseating, so the farmers bred the smugness back in. If the lemon juice doesn't calm down the bitterness enough for your taste, then it's best to only eat pan-fried kale when you are in love.

SESAME-ROASTED
BROCCOLI

Imagine yourself as very tiny—so tiny that stems of broccoli are full-grown trees. Their soft exterior would be grippy enough to climb with spiked shoes and Claw Gloves™, and it would be very romantic to picnic atop the broccoli tops with a napkin blanket and matchbox basket. Part of that romance would involve fighting off beetles with toothpick spears and not dying in the process.

But it might be even more romantic if one of you did die. Eventually, a small shrine would be built at the base of the broccoli tree, honoring the brave fight. You (if you were not the one who died) would walk by, at least once a day, and give a solemn nod. Occasionally, the beetle that won the battle would wander by the shrine and feel a pang of guilt for having such an aggressive nature. "Maybe I can be better," it will think. "Maybe I can do something productive with my life."

Also, while the shrine would be sturdy and built to withstand the seasons, the broccoli would eventually start rotting. Some of the villagers would quietly mutter that it should be burned, while others would say that doing so would be insensitive, even though they would secretly agree.

SERVES 4 (OR 2 ON A SUPER SPECIAL OCCASION CALLED BROCCOLI NIGHT)

3 cups roughly chopped broccoli florets from 1 medium head

1 tablespoon olive oil

1½ tablespoons sesame oil

1 tablespoon sesame seeds

1 teaspoon fine sea salt, plus more to taste

Freshly ground pepper

1 ➜ Preheat the oven to 400°F. Line a baking sheet with parchment paper.

2 ➜ In a large bowl, combine the broccoli, olive oil, sesame oil, sesame seeds, salt, and pepper to taste and wangjangle until evenly coated. Arrange the broccoli on the baking sheet and roast for 20 minutes, until browned.

3 ➜ Remove from the oven and let cool for 5 minutes. Taste and add salt and pepper as needed, then serve.

ROSEMARY
ROASTED POTATOES

Potatoes are a root vegetable. If trees had root vegetables for roots, instead of tree roots, forests would be a distant memory. This thought makes the current tree root situation kind of bittersweet, because those tree root vegetables would probably be pretty delicious.

If potatoes had tree roots for roots instead of potatoes, we probably wouldn't even bother planting them, unless we learned how to make root jerky.

Jerky notwithstanding, I usually prefer my potatoes roasted, as opposed to boiled or raw. They are the best root vegetable to combine with rosemary and coconut oil on account of them being a flavorless black hole. Use one kind of potato, or use many kinds if you're feeling risky.

SERVES 4

3 medium or 4 small potatoes or sweet potatoes, cut into 1-inch cubes

2 tablespoons coconut oil, melted

1 tablespoon chopped fresh rosemary

¾ teaspoon fine sea salt, plus more to taste

Freshly ground pepper

1 → Preheat the oven to 400°F. Line a baking sheet with parchment paper.

2 → In a large bowl, combine the potatoes, coconut oil, rosemary, salt, and pepper to taste and wangjangle until the potatoes are evenly coated. Arrange the potatoes on the prepared baking sheet and roast for 30 minutes, or until the bottoms are browned. Remove the baking sheet from the oven and wrassle the potatoes, then return to the oven and roast for 20 minutes more, until the potatoes are fully cooked and browned on all sides.

3 → Allow to cool to a less than mouth-burning temperature for 10 minutes, add more salt and pepper to taste, then serve.

TOASTED WALNUT CAULIFLOWER STUFF

Cauliflower is hot right now. It's as if everyone suddenly realized that cauliflower isn't just a broccoli-shaped potato. It's actually cauliflower-shaped rice. And it's delicious.

I didn't eat the stuff for years because I tried to grow it once. Well, I was successful with the growing part, but I was unsuccessful with the not-having-pincher-bugs-crawl-out-of-it-when-I-took-it-apart part. And that's the reason you should read this paragraph *after* you make the recipe, rather than before—so you won't be put off of cauliflower.

I also grew tomatoes that summer. Someone once told me that tomatoes need a ton of water to grow. I asked if they could be overwatered. That person said no. So I dug small moats around my tomato plants with channels connecting them, and I left the hose on to drip all day.

I did that for several days.

Have you ever seen a tomato water balloon? Because that's how you get tomato water balloons. They were so watered down they weren't even red anymore. They were a pale, sickly, light orange. They were splitting from being inflated so much. And they were also sitting on the ground from the weight.

I didn't eat tomatoes for a while after that either. And now I leave the vegetable growing to the professionals.

SERVES 2

1 tablespoon olive oil

2 scallions, thinly sliced

2 tablespoons salted butter

3 cups cauliflower florets (from 1 large head)

½ cup walnuts

1 teaspoon honey

½ teaspoon fine sea salt

Freshly ground pepper

Juice of ¼ lemon

1 ➔ In a large nonstick skillet, heat the oil over medium heat until it shimmers like tinsel on a Christmas tree decorated by a seven-year-old. Add the scallions and sauté for 1 minute, until soft. Add the butter and wangjangle until it's melted.

2 ➔ Add the cauliflower, toss to coat it in the butter, and cook for 2 minutes, or until slightly softened. Add the walnuts, honey, salt, and pepper to taste and continue cooking for 8 to 10 minutes, until the cauliflower starts to brown.

3 ➔ Remove the pan from the heat, squeeze the lemon juice over the cauliflower, then serve.

VEGGIES IN
THE FRONT

It wasn't long ago that eating vegetables as a main course was seen as an instant death sentence.

It didn't seem possible that the human body could survive for more than a few minutes without beef. This was when a vegetarian diet was defined as only eating animals that didn't eat other animals. It was a different time. A tougher time.

People didn't drink cow's milk, they drank cow's blood, and they washed it down with gravy. They breathed water instead of air. Not because it was good for them, but because it was bad for them. The fear of hell was the only thing that kept people going, and the only thing that kept people from dying was knowing they wouldn't be able to keep complaining about going to hell if they were dead.

It was a time when the only thing everyone agreed on was how awful being alive was and how stupid everyone was for being born in the first place. A time when nobody acknowledged emotions because there was only one emotion, regret, and only one feeling, extreme discomfort, and people felt as much of both for as long as they were awake—which was almost never, because consciousness was for suckers.

If you got caught being awake, you pretended you were sleeping, and if you got caught pretending to sleep, you accused the other person of being in a dream and crossed your fingers that you could hoodwink your way out of it.

Arteries were so clogged with lard that people could barely move their limbs. Stretching hadn't been invented yet, and even if it had, people didn't have the patience for it and would have punched you in the face for trying if they had been flexible enough to make a fist.

It was a simpler time. A predictable time. And people were happily hating it. Then vegetables came along and ruined everything. Beef was no longer just good enough on its own. Now you had to spend time growing things, and since there were more things to eat, there wasn't enough cow's blood and gravy to wash everything down.

People started breathing air and drinking water and even stretching became normal. Schools were built, people had fun, and that's how we ended up with the utopia we enjoy throughout the world today. All thanks to vegetables.

SIMPLE
STIR-FRY

The Stir-Fry is one of the few dishes where the instructions to make it are embedded in the name. You stir it while frying. We're pretty lucky that all foods aren't a description of the cooking process. Soup would be a nice hot bowl of Stir-Boiled. An omelet would be a Fry Flip. Popcorn would be Hot Poppity Pot Chaos. Or Flippity Poppity Corn. Or Firecracker Snackerjacks. Oh wait, it seems popcorn already has the instructions embedded in its name. Well, now we know there's room for improvement.

SERVES 2

2 tablespoons vegetable, canola, or peanut oil

1 garlic clove, finely chopped

1 tablespoon finely chopped fresh ginger

1 medium yellow onion, thinly sliced

1 cup carrot matchsticks (from 1 medium carrot)

1 red bell pepper, cut into strips

1 cup roughly chopped broccoli

1 tablespoon soy sauce

2 tablespoons orange juice

1 teaspoon sesame oil (optional)

Cooked rice of your choice, for serving

1 → In a large pan or wok, heat the vegetable oil over medium-high heat until it shimmers like a goblet full of jewels in a treasure chest on a pirate's ship that you found legally and therefore can keep the booty. Add the garlic and ginger and sauté, moving them around with an air of self-confidence, for 1 minute, until softened. Increase the heat to high, add the onion, carrot, bell pepper, and broccoli and cook for 1 minute, until they are well coated with oil.

2 → Add the soy sauce, orange juice, and sesame oil (if using) and continue wangjangling the vegetables for 2 to 3 minutes more, until they are slightly softened but crisp.

3 → Remove the stir-fry from the pan and serve with rice.

NOTES

Carrots are the densest vegetable in this dish, which is why you want them cut thinner than the onions, so you can cook them both at the same time. If slicing into matchsticks is too much work, just slice them similarly to the onions and add them to the pan 1 minute earlier.

The reason we don't talk about the thicknesses of peppers is because their thickness is determined by God. But we can talk about their widths, since those are determined by your knife (which was created by God, but let's not get into that). Just make them a bit wider than they are thick.

We *never* talk about the thickness of broccoli. And you should know better than to ask.

The sesame oil takes the edge off the sweetness of the orange juice and makes the dish more savory. It's good both ways, so just flip a coin, or maybe even consult your own taste buds to determine the best course of action.

STUFFED PEPPERS

I think using the word "stuffed" might be overstating things here. You're not going to stuff the peppers so much as you're going to fill them. Maybe you'll lightly pack them. But "stuffing" is probably a slightly too aggressive word to describe the process of filling the vacant pepper chamber with fluffed cauliflower snow.

SERVES 1

1 cup cauliflower rice
(from ¼ head)

1 scallion, thinly sliced

½ cup grated parmesan cheese

1 garlic clove, grated or minced

½ teaspoon red wine vinegar

¼ teaspoon fine sea salt

1 large bell pepper, stem end sliced off, cored, and seeded

1 ➡ Preheat the oven to 400°F. Line a baking sheet with parchment paper.

2 ➡ In a large bowl, combine the cauliflower, scallion, one-third of the parmesan, the garlic, red wine vinegar, and salt and wang-jangle thoroughly. Place the pepper upright on the prepared baking sheet and spoon the mixture into it until it is full. Top with the remaining parmesan.

3 ➡ Bake the pepper for about 40 minutes, or until the cheese on top starts to brown. Remove from the oven, slice the pepper in half vertically and transfer to a plate as two steaming, hand-crafted, open-faced, cauliflower pepper bowls. If you're really not too hungry, give half to a friend. Otherwise eat both halves in front of an enemy.

NOTES

Remember when I said to spoon the mixture into the pepper? I didn't type that out just to entertain myself. I said it because you're gonna be tempted to tilt the bowl and dump it in. Then a glob of cauliflower is gonna fall onto the pan and you're gonna look like a friggin' rookie. And you're gonna look like a friggin' rookie because if you do that, you *are* a friggin' rookie. And then, buddy, let me tell you, you'll be in a world of pain. Not physical pain. The psychological pain of realizing you're a rookie.

Baking times are gonna vary here so keep an eye on it. If that cheese really starts browning, get it out of the oven, but not before then.

To turn your cauliflower into rice, you have a few options: (1) buy it that way to begin with, (2) use a hand-grater, (3) use a food processor, (4) become a magician.

Remember when I was talking about being a rookie earlier? There's nothing wrong with that. Nobody should rook-shame anybody. Everyone starts somewhere. The only reason I know you should use a spoon is because I tried to tilt the bowl and dump the cauliflower into the pepper, and a glob of cauliflower fell onto the pan. Which just goes to show I'm really only mad at myself.

ZUCCHINI BUTTER NOODLES

The war against pasta has been going strong for the past few years. Pasta makers are nervous. Flour tycoons are furious. And noodle addicts wonder if there will be anything left to eat in a decade. Those who enjoy both pasta and noodle-shaped vegetables live in fear of having to pick a side. Hopefully things will settle down, soon. In the meanwhile, it's a good idea to learn how to make, and eat, alternative noodles, in case pasta is soon extinct. But it's also a good idea to learn how to eat pasta in case noodle-shaped vegetables are soon outlawed.

SERVES 2

2 teaspoons olive oil

3 tablespoons salted butter

3 garlic cloves, finely chopped

4 cups zucchini noodles from two small-medium zucchinis

Grated parmesan cheese

1 → In a large nonstick skillet, heat the oil and butter over medium heat. When the butter is melted, add the garlic and cook for 2 minutes, stirring constantly, until softened.

2 → Add the zucchini noodles, tossing to coat them, then reduce the heat to medium-low and cook for 3 minutes, while stirring, until the noodles are softened.

3 → Transfer the noodles to a plate, add as much parmesan as you like, and enjoy. Or eat them begrudgingly.

NOTES

You can buy zucchini noodles, or you can make your own with a julienne slicer, a spiralizer, or a mandoline slicer.

If you use a julienne slicer, lay your zucchini flat on your cutting board and drag the slicer down the length of the zucchini and away from your hand.

If you're going to get one tool specifically for making zucchini noodles, I recommend the spiralizer. Certain types of spiralizers core the middle of the veggie, removing the seeds, and leaving less water in your noodles.

If you want something more versatile for slicing a variety of vegetables in different ways, the mandoline slicer is a great choice. If you want something less versatile for slicing a variety of vegetables in different ways, the chainsaw is a great option. It also usually results in you having the kitchen to yourself whenever you use it.

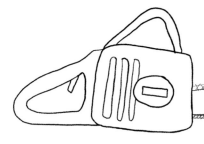
CHAINMASTERZZZ™

NEARLY SAUCELESS PASTA

I used to be against any pasta that wasn't drowning in sauce. Pasta was simply the delivery system for tomato, meat, cream, or any other kind of sauce. And lots of it. If I couldn't drink it, I didn't want to eat it. Perhaps I have matured. Or perhaps my tastes have expanded. Or maybe I have simply realized that what I lack in sauce can be made up for with parmesan cheese.

SERVES 4

½ tablespoon fine sea salt

½ pound fettuccine

¼ cup olive oil

2 garlic cloves, finely chopped

2 scallions, thinly sliced

1 red bell pepper, sliced

2 cups grape or cherry tomatoes, halved or quartered

½ cup Kalamata olives, sliced

½ teaspoon crushed red pepper

Grated parmesan cheese, for serving

Freshly ground pepper

1 ➜ Fill a large saucepan with 10 cups water, add the salt, and bring to a boil over high heat. Add the pasta and let the water return to a boil. Reduce the heat to medium-high and cook for 8 to 10 minutes, until the pasta is al dente, or slightly firm to the bite.

2 ➜ Meanwhile, in a large nonstick skillet, heat the oil over medium heat until it shimmers like a freshly waxed Rolls-Royce under a moonlit disco ball. Add the garlic and cook for 1 minute, until soft.

3 ➜ Add the scallions and cook for 1 minute while stirring. Don't cry. Add the bell pepper, tomatoes, olives, and crushed red pepper. Don't laugh. Cook for 8 to 10 minutes, or until the bell pepper is softened and the tomatoes are wilting. Reduce the heat to low.

4 ➜ Set aside ¼ cup of the pasta cooking water, drain the pasta, and add the pasta to the skillet with the veggies. Add the pasta cooking water to the skillet and wangjangle until fully combined.

5 ➜ Divide the pasta and veggies among four plates or bowls and top with parmesan cheese and pepper to taste.

NOTES

This pasta isn't going to mix super great. It's like the emulsion of pastas. When serving, use your tongs to grab some of the noodles, and then some of the vegetables, as it's hard to grip them together. In the future, where grippy tomatoes are ubiquitous, this isn't a problem.

If you're serving this dish to others, don't selfishly take the plate with the most tomatoes and olives. But if you *are* going to do that, bury some inside a mound of pasta so the portions look equal.

If you're just making it for yourself, divide the portions evenly, because if you put more of the good stuff in the portion you eat immediately, you'll only be screwing over your future self. But maybe your future self deserves that because of your past selfish behavior.

PANIC-FRIED

BLACK BEANS AND RICE

This recipe uses one of my favorite things to eat in the world: food. One hundred percent of the ingredients of this dish are food based, which makes it almost completely edible. Beans and rice are two of the most versatile edible substances as well. They can be flavored with nearly anything, cooked in a variety of ways, and almost everybody likes them.

There's no consensus on how to handle someone who doesn't like rice and beans, but I recommend feeling pity. And then bring yourself back to gratitude because your portion just doubled.

SERVES 2 TO 4

FOR THE RICE

1 cup long-grain white rice

1 teaspoon fine sea salt

FOR THE BEANS

3 tablespoons olive oil

1 small red onion, diced (about 2 cups)

1 jalapeño pepper, seeded and diced

1 (15.5-ounce) can black beans, drained and rinsed

1½ tablespoons ground cumin

1 teaspoon chili powder

¾ teaspoon fine sea salt

1 → Make the rice: In a small saucepan, combine the rice and salt with 1½ cups water and bring to a boil over high heat. Reduce the heat to low, cover, and cook for 20 minutes, or until the water has been completely absorbed. Uncover and fluff the rice with a fork.

2 → Meanwhile, make the beans: In a medium skillet, heat the olive oil over medium heat until it shimmers like the tinfoil T-shirt you made for Halloween that one year when you thought you looked like a cool robot but you actually looked like crumpled garbage. Add the onion and jalapeño and cook for about 8 minutes, or until the onion starts to brown. Add the beans, cumin, chili powder, and salt and wangjangle until it's so dry you almost panic.

3 → Don't panic. Add ½ cup water, mix thoroughly, then cook until the mixture thickens, about 3 minutes.

4 → Move the rice and beans to a plate, then move that plate to your mouth. Or use a fork.

NOTES

After you cut the jalapeño in half, use a spoon to scrape the insides out. You can get it in one deft swoop, even taking the stem off with a most impressive stroke. Now don't touch anyone's eyeballs until after you wash your hands.

If your pepper prep went as well as I just described, brag about it on social media until your rice and beans get cold.

SURPRISE: They're good at every temperature.

LOADED CAULIFLOWER BAKE

The word "loaded" is very cool. It's the kind of word that gives you that *being bad* feeling, even though you're not being bad at all. You're baking cauliflower.

It's nice to have an opportunity to give a word like "loaded" a positive association, as most of us have spent too much time waiting for things to load. That's what's great about books: no loading. Just reading. You can also incorporate the word into other activities in your life to give you a safe thrill. Such as "loaded toast," which is toast with butter on top, "loaded tea," which is tea with both milk *and* sugar in it, and "loaded walking," which is walking around while wearing clothing.

But make sure you don't make loaded cauliflower while you are loaded, or the effect of both will be canceled out.

SERVES 2

FOR THE CAULIFLOWER

3 cups bite-sized chunks cauliflower

1 yellow bell pepper, cut into bite-sized pieces

2 scallions, thinly sliced

½ (15.5-ounce) can black beans, drained and rinsed

1½ tablespoons salted butter, melted

1 tablespoon olive oil

½ teaspoon fine sea salt

FOR THE CHEESE SAUCE

1 cup grated cheddar cheese

4 ounces cream cheese, at room temperature

½ cup 2% milk

½ tablespoon chili garlic sauce

1 → Preheat the oven to 450°F. Line a 9-inch square baking dish with parchment paper. (See Notes.)

2 → Make the cauliflower: In a large bowl, combine the cauliflower, bell pepper, scallions, black beans, melted butter, olive oil, and salt and toss until everything is mixed thoroughly and evenly coated. Transfer the mixture to the prepared dish and bake for about 45 minutes, or until the cauliflower and pepper start to brown.

3 → Meanwhile, make the cheese sauce: In a small saucepan, heat the cheddar, cream cheese, milk, and chili garlic sauce over medium-low heat, wangjangling occasionally, for about 6 minutes, or until everything is combined smoothly. Feel free to substitute another hot sauce of your choice for the chili garlic sauce.

4 → Remove the veggies from the oven and pour the cheese elixir on top while uttering an incantation. Alternatively, you can dole out the servings to individual plates, then apply the cheese ointment to each one based on personal cheese-sauce tolerance levels while uttering the Hippocratic Oath.

(RECIPE CONTINUES)

NOTES

If you don't have a square baking dish, go ahead and use a baking sheet lined with parchment paper instead. It will take a bit less time to cook because the ingredients will be more flattened out, so keep an eye on it and trust the browning more than the timing. I mean, trust the browning regardless of the option you choose.

If you're feeling ambitious, you can cut cauliflower into slices, like thick tortilla chips. I'm not sure this will be any better, but I know you "can" do it. Lemme know how that goes if you take the road less traveled.

Did you know that "I took the one less traveled by, and that has made all the difference," from that famous poem is largely misinterpreted? I don't have time to explain it, but look it up. It's kind of neat.

VEGGIE RICE BOWL

Vegetables. Rice. A bowl. What more could you want in a meal? Don't answer that. If you ask yourself that question every time you make something, you'll be overwhelmed with FOMO.

Instead, ask yourself this: Do I like easy things? If you answered yes, then consider ordering takeout instead of making this. Because while this dish isn't especially difficult, it will still take you a few minutes to make and time is always at a premium.

SERVES 2

FOR THE RICE

½ cup basmati rice

½ tablespoon salted butter

FOR THE DRESSING

1½ teaspoons grated fresh ginger

3 tablespoons olive oil

1 tablespoon rice vinegar

1 teaspoon honey

¼ teaspoon fine sea salt

½ teaspoon sesame oil

FOR THE VEGGIES

1 cup thinly sliced cucumber

½ cup thinly sliced carrot

1 cup thinly sliced red bell pepper

1 avocado, sliced

1 → Make the rice: In a small saucepan, combine the rice, ¾ cup water, and butter and bring to a boil over high heat. Reduce the heat to low, cover, and simmer for 15 minutes. Remove the saucepan from the heat and let it sit, still covered, for 10 minutes, until all the water has been absorbed. Remove the lid and fluff the rice with a fork.

2 → Meanwhile, make the dressing: In a small bowl, combine the ginger, olive oil, rice vinegar, honey, salt, and sesame oil and stir ferociously.

3 → Divide the rice between two bowls, then divide the vegetables between the bowls in pleasing configurations that may or may not send a secret message to your loved one.

4 → Wangjangle the dressing vigorously again, then divide the dressing between the veggies in each bowl and serve.

NOTES

Sending secret messages to your loved one with sliced vegetables is not the most efficient way to communicate. The most efficient way to communicate is with abstract mouth sounds that are interpreted as "ideas." The vegetables, however, give you a rare opportunity to be passive-aggressive without being called out on it. One misplaced cucumber, which shatters the otherwise perfect symmetry of the presentation, can make someone feel mildly awkward, and might be enough of a personal victory to get you through one more night.

When you're lying in bed thinking of all the things you would say if you weren't afraid to communicate, consider trying to say them out loud, then become paralyzed with fear.

Please note, though, that sending a secret message to yourself with subliminal vegetables is not recommended as you may end up becoming perpetually suspicious of yourself.

MEAT, SOME FISH,

AND
MOSTLY
CHICKEN

Meat comes from animals—or at least it used to. Over the past few years, scientists have been busy growing meat inside labs, the same way we grow our nonheirloom children. Those of us heirloom humans, while slower, weaker, and less intelligent than the nonheirlooms, are also emotionally erratic, more condescending, and way more delicious.

One of the greatest challenges lab-meat scientists have been facing is how to make lab meat taste like real meat.

Recent discoveries indicate that much of the flavor that comes from animal meat is related not only to the animal's diet, but also to its memories and emotions. Double-blind tests show that lab steak that has been made to watch 100 hours of videos of cows grazing in a pasture with dappled sunlight, mooing sounds, and an occasional car driving down the nearby dusty road, tastes up to 17 percent better than lab meat that only spends its time with boring scientists.

In Scandinavia, meat scientists have found an improvement in the lab-chicken flavor when they dress in brightly colored pants with sparkling wigs and thigh-high leather boots—at least, they've found this when they consume the chicken while wearing those clothes and are intoxicated.

In another experiment, lab sausage that was taken to an amusement park once a week to ride the roller coasters and eat funnel cake was significantly tastier than the control group, even when most of the frosting was removed. And in yet another case, lab meat that had been genetically engineered to fall in love with other lab meat was the tastiest of all. This experiment, of course, brought up a whole other set of ethical issues, such as:

Why waste falling-in-love technology on lab meat when it could be used on dogs?

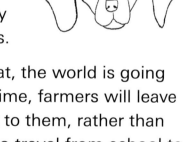

Scientists have yet to attempt making lab fish because they are too slippery to handle safely in a scientific environment. They are addressing this by genetically engineering grippy hands.

When lab meat replaces farmed meat, the world is going to be a different place. For the first time, farmers will leave their land and we will be able to talk to them, rather than just the actors that play farmers who travel from school to school promoting Food Pyramid propaganda. It's going to be wild.

You might be terrified to try cooking meat and fish things. I know I was. These sorts of foods can kill you if you don't cook them properly. Uncooked chicken can give you salmonella, which can cause you to die in a matter of seconds;

undercooked steak can give you a good trampling, which can cause you to die in a matter of minutes; and undercooked fish is usually only lethal when it's a shark attacking you. What I'm saying is you want to make sure you cook this stuff the right amount. If you're new to the game, consider getting an instant-read thermometer. Cooking meat, chicken, and fish to specific internal temperatures is the safest way to know you have killed any potentially harmful bacteria. Many people simply rely on visual and textural cues to determine whether or not meat and fish are cooked through, along with just plain old-fashioned guts. (Their guts, not the animal's.) Affirmative statements such as "Yup, that's done," or "Yup, she's cooked alright," are also helpful in giving your body a placebo-induced immune boost, which can swing the scales in your favor if your stomach ever needs to wage war on something potentially harmful. Or you can at least tell yourself that.

COOKING TIMES

After cooking meat, chicken, or fish a couple of times at the same temperature, you will get familiar enough with your stovetop or Kitchen Hot Box to know how it's going to turn out. Pay attention to the temperature setting and time and adjust as necessary as you figure out what you like best.

Everyone has a preference in relation to how well done they like their steak. I prefer mine medium-rare. Some people who have never had a medium-rare steak think they prefer medium. And some people who have never had medium-rare or medium steak think they prefer well-done. The choice is yours with zero judgment out loud.

Cook your steak to an internal temperature of about 130°F for medium-rare, around 140°F for medium, around 150°F for medium-well, and around 160°F for no thanks.

The USDA recommends cooking beef to a minimum of 145°F, but almost anyone who knows anything about anything thinks anything higher than this is overcooked. But if that's the way you like it, don't listen to anyone who knows anything about anything. If the temperature of your steak is around 101.5°F, it means the steak you are about to eat is actually a live cow. Enjoy.

The safe internal temperature for chicken is 165°F. Cook your chicken so that the thickest part hits this temperature and try to minimize how much it goes over so that it remains tender and moist. Remember that carryover of the heat may cause the temperature to rise a few degrees after you stop cooking. Also, in numerology, 165 is a very lucky number but anything higher than that is so unlucky it could destroy your life, so proceed with caution.

The safe internal temperature for fish is 145°F and this is usually indicated when it flakes easily with a fork. In numerology, 145 is the Number of the Bison, which is simply confusing.

SIMPLE
SMEARED CHICKEN BREAST

This is almost as simple as it gets. It could have been called Entry Level Chicken. Or Chicken with Almost Nothing. Or Chicken for Babies.

The smearing mediums we will use for this recipe are hummus and mustard. Hummus gives more of a subtle, creamy chicken experience while mustard provides more of a spiced, yellow chicken experience. The wide variety of available hummus flavors allows you to season the chicken according to your mood. And mustard allows you the thrilling experience of walking the will-I-stain-my-pants tightrope.

Mustard isn't something you might commonly associate with chicken. That's only because people don't usually put mustard on chicken. But I do. Or at least I did. I'm a little bit too busy eating other things right now to do it at this moment, but I probably will in the future.

There are a lot of different spellings of the word "hummus" in English, including "humous,"" houmous," "hummus," and "humus," which is also the word for rotting wood.

One might argue that "houmous" is a superior spelling of the word because it has two unnecessary o's, which make it appear fancier, and hummus deserves to be fancy. Some might argue that sneaking extra vowels into the word is a waste of letters, and that we should consider the impact those two unnecessary o's will have on the environment and therefore on the future of humanity.

If the word "houmous" is written 6 quadrillion times over the next several years, it will be enough to fill 279,955,207,166.8 pages of Internet paper, which is wasteful. The only solution that makes sense is to use the more efficient "hms" when referring to this delicious food, which will save us oodles of googlebytes.

No matter what you smear on your chicken breast, be careful to smear it thoroughly all around the chicken, but be extra careful not to smear the chicken's reputation.

SERVES 2

2 (5-ounce) boneless skinless chicken breasts

Fine sea salt and freshly ground pepper

2 tablespoons whole-grain mustard or 3 tablespoons hummus

1 ➔ Preheat the oven to 400°F. Line a baking sheet with parchment paper.

2 ➔ Place the chicken breasts on the baking sheet and season to taste with salt and pepper on both sides. Smear the chicken all over with either the mustard or the hummus and set aside to marinate for about 40 minutes.

3 ➔ Bake the chicken for 20 minutes, or until the chicken is cooked through (an instant-read thermometer inserted in the thickest part of the breast should read 165°F). Remove the chicken from the oven and allow it to cool for 10 minutes before serving.

NOTES

This recipe works best with chicken breasts that aren't too thick. Keep it under an inch.

This recipe also works best with a mustard containing grains that are under an inch thick, which is all mustards, so no need to worry about that.

MAPLE-BAKED
SALMON

I love salmon so much that it's almost exclusively the only kind of fish I cook (which I do at least once every two years). Why bother learning how to make something else when you've already discovered perfection? Because perfection is boring and childish. Discovering new things, while risky and time consuming, is also fun and occasionally rewarding.

Some pro tips: You can tell when salmon is cooked through when it's gone from translucent to opaque, and it easily flakes with a fork. If you take the salmon out just before it's cooked through, the carryover of the heat may be enough to finish it in the middle after a few minutes. Barely cooked salmon is the best, in my opinion, which is the opinion of someone who knows how best to cook salmon (also known as me). If the salmon is flipping and flopping around in the marinade, do not be alarmed. This is just a joyful muscle-memory reflex that sometimes happens when the fish comes back into contact with liquid. It feels like it is back home for a few seconds before remembering that it's actually dead.

SERVES 2

1 tablespoon olive oil

1 tablespoon maple syrup

½ teaspoon soy sauce

1 garlic clove, grated

1-inch piece fresh ginger, grated

2 (6-ounce) salmon fillets

1 ➔ Preheat the oven to 400°F. Line a baking sheet with parchment paper.

2 ➔ In a shallow medium bowl, combine the olive oil, maple syrup, soy sauce, garlic, and ginger and stir thoroughly. Place the salmon fillets skin side up in the marinade and set aside to marinate for about 25 minutes at room temperature.

3 ➔ Arrange the fillets skin side down on the prepared baking sheet, spread a teaspoon of marinade on top of each fillet, and use a fork to add more of the ginger and garlic from the marinade if you wish. Bake for 15 to 25 minutes, until the salmon is cooked through to medium doneness. Check with a fork that the fish is flaking in the middle, or use an instant-read thermometer to check that it has reached 145°F.

4 ➔ Remove the salmon from the oven and allow to cool for 10 minutes before serving.

BAKED
TILAPIA
WITH DILL

The word "tilapia" doesn't sound like it's a type of fish, unless you've been conditioned by Big Dictionary to think that way. It sounds more like a shiny, expensive teapot. For example: "Honey, the Galloways are coming for dinner, would you mind polishing the tilapia?"

It also sounds like a fragile foot bone. If I may: "We just got the results back, and I don't think you're gonna like them. Your tilapia has shattered into three thousand pieces."

It also sounds like a condition that causes you to have someone else's daydreams. As in: "Whenever I drift off, I imagine I'm hand crafting a book shelf in a carpenter's workshop, but I'm afraid of wood. My tilapia must be worse that I thought."

But the truth is that tilapia is just a boring old fish that's pretty light on flavor—it tends to take on the taste of whatever you cook it with, which is why we combine the most boring fish with the most interesting weed: dill.

SERVES 2

2 (6-ounce) boneless skinless tilapia fillets

Fine sea salt and freshly ground pepper

2 tablespoons salted butter, melted

2 teaspoons dried dill

1 garlic clove, pressed or minced

Juice of ⅛ lemon

1 ➜ Preheat the oven to 400°F. Line a baking sheet with parchment paper.

2 ➜ Place the fillets on the baking sheet and season both sides with salt and pepper, allowing the fillets to come up to room temperature for about half an hour.

3 ➜ Meanwhile, in a small bowl, combine the butter, dill, and garlic, wangjangling thoroughly, and allow the flavors to infuse for a few minutes.

4 ➜ Stir the butter mixture again, then spoon it over the tilapia to cover it completely, and allow it to sit for about 10 minutes (which can be part of the half hour temperature-raising time—there is a lot of resting in this recipe and it's for your own benefit).

5 ➜ Bake the tilapia for 10 to 15 minutes, until it is cooked through to medium doneness. Use a fork to check that the fish is flaking in the middle or use an instant-read thermometer to confirm that it has reached an internal temperature of 145°F at the thickest part.

6 ➜ Squeeze the lemon on the fish, and serve with a side of tea poured from your shiny tilapia.

SAUSAGE AND CHICKPEA CURRY

The first-ever sausage joke was cracked in Hardinsburg, Kentucky, in 1957 and was received with a halfhearted snort. By the 1960s, sausage jokes had taken America by storm, but they went out of fashion by 1973. The 1980s saw sausage humor make a tepid comeback, and the 1990s were a very sausage-dense time in the comedy world. But when the 2000s hit, it seemed that sausage jokes had almost gone extinct.

Market research shows that including sausage jokes in this book won't significantly increase sales, because cookbook buyers are a sophisticated bunch, and sausage jokes are low-hanging fruit.

SERVES 4

4 links Italian sausage

2 tablespoons olive oil

1 large red or yellow onion, diced

2 red bell peppers, sliced

1 (13.5-ounce) can coconut milk

2 to 3 tablespoons Indian curry paste of choice

1 teaspoon brown sugar

½ teaspoon fine sea salt

1 (15.5-ounce) can chickpeas, drained and rinsed

Freshly ground black pepper

Rice, for serving (optional)

Chopped cilantro or parsley, for garnish (optional)

1 ➜ Preheat the oven to 400°F. Line a baking sheet with parchment paper.

2 ➜ Arrange the sausages on the baking sheet and bake for 15 minutes, or until almost cooked through.

3 ➜ Meanwhile, in a medium saucepan, heat the olive oil over medium heat until it shimmers like a desert mirage on a nice sunny day when you're out of water and close to death and wish you would have just followed the goddamn map in the first place. Add the onion and cook, stirring, for 2 minutes, or until slightly softened.

4 ➜ Add the bell peppers and continue cooking for 5 minutes, or until the peppers start to soften and the onions turn golden. Add the coconut milk, curry paste, brown sugar, salt, and chickpeas and wangjangle until combined.

5 ➜ Remove the sausages from the oven and cut into ½-inch slices. Add the sausage to the saucepan and wangjangle until submerged, using the opposite hand you used for the first wangjangling to make it taste less predictable.

6 ➜ Reduce the heat to medium-low and simmer, stirring occasionally, for 15 to 20 minutes, until the sausages are cooked through and the sauce has thickened. Add black pepper to taste. Serve the curry on its own, or on top of rice. Add a small handful of chopped cilantro or parsley if you want something fresh, herby, and green.

NOTES

Indian curry pastes vary in heat level, strength, and flavor, so you'll have to taste it out and adjust the amount in your dish accordingly. If you think it's strong, start with 2 tablespoons and add more until you nearly pass out because it tastes so perfect.

Clean the kitchen during the simmering phase. When you're in a hot sausage curry coma, you'll be so glad you did, and you won't be mad that you didn't.

If cilantro tastes like soap to you, you can cancel this effect by washing your mouth out with soap before you eat it.

LEEKY OLIVE
CHICKEN

The way I came up with this recipe is pretty interesting. It was a cold, rainy night. I had a craving for leeks, olives, chicken, and salsa, all cooked together in a skillet, served hot. So I went out and I bought leeks, olives, chicken, and salsa. Then I cooked them together in a skillet until they were hot. Then I ate them. It tasted really good because it was exactly what I wanted. I felt satisfied.

I lied about the part where the way I came up with this recipe was pretty interesting. It wasn't interesting. It was not interesting. What's interesting is that this dish has become one of my favorite things to eat. I hope you're interested.

SERVES 3

1 pound boneless skinless chicken breasts (2 or 3)

Fine sea salt and freshly ground pepper

3 tablespoons olive oil

2 medium leeks, sliced (4 to 5 cups)

1 cup chopped Kalamata olives

1½ cups mild or medium salsa

Rice, orzo, or quinoa, for serving (optional)

1 → Preheat the oven to 400°F. Line a baking sheet with parchment paper.

2 → Place the chicken breasts on the prepared baking sheet and season generously with salt and pepper, then drizzle ½ tablespoon olive oil over them. Flip the chicken breasts and repeat with salt, pepper, and another ½ tablespoon of oil. Allow them to marinate at room temperature for about 40 minutes.

3 → Bake the chicken for 15 minutes, or until they are almost but not quite cooked through.

4 → Meanwhile, in a large nonstick skillet, heat the remaining 2 tablespoons olive oil over medium heat until it shimmers like the chrome on a motorcycle that does not look cool because the dude is revving it loudly like a moron. Add the leeks and cook, wangjangling regularly, for 7 minutes, or until they become soft.

5 → Remove the chicken from the oven and cut it into bite-sized pieces. Add the chicken, olives, and salsa to the skillet with the leeks and simmer for 10 minutes, while wangjangling, until the chicken is cooked through and no longer pink.

6 → Season with salt and pepper to taste. Serve on its own or over rice, orzo, or quinoa.

MEAT AND POTATOES

Potatoes and beef are like two peas in a pod. Or, like one thing that came out of the dirt and one thing that grew up in a barn. They've lived different lives. They've had different experiences. But the one thing they have in common is the ground. They both needed it to survive. Without it, they would have just been floating in space, and would have quickly suffocated due to the lack of oxygen. They may not know each other, or even understand each other, but when they're on the plate together, the ground is the one thing they can both appreciate.

SERVES 2 TO 4

FOR THE POTATOES

2 large russet potatoes

2 teaspoons olive oil

Fine sea salt and freshly ground pepper

2 tablespoons salted butter

2 garlic cloves, pressed

FOR THE BEEF

2 tablespoons olive oil

1 medium red onion, chopped

1 pound 85% lean ground beef

2 tablespoons chili powder

2 tablespoons red wine vinegar

2 teaspoons honey

¾ teaspoon fine sea salt

Freshly ground pepper

1 → Preheat the oven to 400°F. Line a baking sheet with parchment paper.

2 → Make the potatoes: Place the potatoes on the baking sheet, poke some fork holes all over them, then drizzle them with the olive oil and rub all over until they're evenly coated. Season with salt and pepper on all sides.

3 → Bake the potatoes for about 1 hour, or until a fork slides in easily. Remove the potatoes from the oven, and using a fork to handle them and avoid the steam, halve them lengthwise. Scoop the insides of the potatoes into a medium bowl, reserving the skins. Add the butter, garlic, and more salt and pepper to the bowl and mash thoroughly with a fork or hand masher.

4 → Meanwhile, make the beef: In a large nonstick skillet, heat the oil over medium-high heat until it shimmers like the Arctic Ocean during narwhal mating season. Add the onion and cook, stirring, for 7 minutes, or until it starts to brown.

5 → Add the beef and break it up into small pieces with your wangjangler, mixing it in thoroughly with the onion and oil. Mix in the chili powder, vinegar, honey, salt, and pepper to taste. Cook for 7 to 10 minutes, until any liquid has evaporated and the beef is browned.

6 → Spoon the hot beef mixture into the potato skins, and serve with mashed potatoes on the side while sitting on the ground.

CURRY CHICKEN
THIGHS

Curry is a complex combination of herbs and spices that originated in India. Much like hot sauce, it is as dangerous as a drug in terms of its addiction potential. I have to physically restrain myself from putting curry in everything I cook, which makes things difficult because cooking while restrained is physically limiting. On a mental and emotional level, however, it's quite expansive. Which is why I highly recommend developing a Level 9 curry addiction.

SERVES 2 OR 3

¼ cup full-fat Greek yogurt

1 tablespoon Dijon mustard

1 tablespoon Indian curry paste of choice

1 teaspoon fine sea salt

1 teaspoon maple syrup

6 boneless skinless chicken thighs (about 1 pound)

Rice or quinoa, for serving

1 → Preheat the oven to 400°F. Line a baking sheet with parchment paper.

2 → In a medium bowl, combine the yogurt, Dijon mustard, curry paste, salt, and maple syrup and wangjangle until well mixed. Add the chicken thighs and turn to coat evenly, making sure to get the marinade in the folds. Set aside to marinate at room temperature for about 30 minutes.

3 → Place the chicken thighs on the prepared baking sheet. Bake for about 20 minutes, or until they are cooked through (an instant-read thermometer inserted in the thickest part of the thigh should read 165°F).

4 → Allow the chicken to cool for 10 minutes before serving with rice, quinoa, or another batch of chicken thighs.

JALAPEÑO CHICKEN
BREAST

There's a lot of chicken breast in this book, but I made this dish spontaneously one night and my roommate's praise was so flattering that I was convinced it was good. I hope that's true because I haven't made it since. Or have I?

You really can't trust something just because it's written in a book. Or can you?

You can, because if someone writes something in a book that isn't truthful, they open themselves up to legal action if somebody feels like they have been deceived. Or do they?

The only way to find out is to lawyer up.

SERVES 2

FOR THE CHICKEN

2 (5-ounce) boneless skinless chicken breasts

Fine sea salt and freshly ground pepper

2 teaspoons olive oil

FOR THE SAUCE

2 tablespoons olive oil

2 jalapeño peppers, seeded and diced

2 shallots, diced

2 cups chopped vine-ripened tomatoes

1 teaspoon brown sugar

½ teaspoon fine sea salt

Freshly ground pepper

5 fresh basil leaves, chopped

1 ➜ Preheat the oven to 400°F. Line a baking sheet with parchment paper.

2 ➜ Make the chicken: Place the chicken breasts on the prepared baking sheet, season with salt and pepper on both sides, then let the chicken marinate at room temperature for 30 to 45 minutes.

3 ➜ Coat the chicken evenly with the olive oil. Bake for 20 minutes, or until cooked through (an instant-read thermometer inserted in the thickest part of the breast should read 165°F).

4 ➜ Meanwhile, make the sauce: In a nonstick medium skillet, heat the olive oil over medium-high heat until it shimmers like a fake Rolex under a buzzing fluorescent light. Add the jalapeños and shallots and cook, wangjangling for 2 minutes, or until softened. Add the tomatoes, brown sugar, salt, and pepper to taste. Cook for 6 minutes, stirring, until the sauce is thickened. Stir in the basil leaves and cook for 1 minute more.

5 ➜ Remove the chicken breasts from the oven, plate them, and cover with the sauce, dividing evenly. Serve hot. Also serve spicy.

PAN-SEARED STRIP LOIN

WITH HORSERADICAL SPINACH

Horseradish was originally part of the Horse Riding Navigation System (HRNS) before we started relying on GPS. Horse drivers would sprinkle horseradish on the ground as they rode, so that the horses could sniff their way back. They soon realized this was a waste of perfectly delicious horseradish since they only rode along clearly marked trails and roads, and not very smart because the horseradish attracted packs of hungry, horse-hating wolves.

While this is the only recipe in the book that calls for horseradish, I have been thinking it would go great in the Creamy Raw Broccoli Salad (page 125). I just KNOW it would taste excellent if you added 1 tablespoon in place of the sesame oil. But the raw broccoli salad is already good, as is. But the horseradish version would be even better.

Anyway, let's get back to our regularly scheduled steak programming.

SERVES 2

FOR THE STEAK

2 (8-ounce) boneless strip loin steaks, 1 inch thick

Fine sea salt and freshly ground pepper

1 tablespoon vegetable oil

FOR THE HORSERADICAL SPINACH

1 tablespoon olive oil

1 tablespoon salted butter

5 ounces baby spinach

1 tablespoon horseradish

1 ➜ Make the steaks: Season both sides of the steaks generously with salt and pepper. Allow it to marinate at room temperature for 30 to 45 minutes.

2 ➜ In a large stainless steel or cast-iron skillet, heat the oil over medium-high heat until it just starts to smoke. Using metal tongs, gently lay the steaks in the skillet away from you, being careful to avoid oil spatter. Cook the steak for 2½ minutes, or until a golden-brown crust has formed on the bottom, then flip them carefully, and cook for another 2½ minutes, until the beautiful crust is duplicated on what is now the new bottom. Turn the steak on its side to cook the fat for 20 seconds, until some of the fat has rendered.

3 ➜ Move the steaks to a cutting board and let them rest while you cook the spinach.

4 ➜ In a large nonstick skillet, heat the olive oil and butter together over medium heat until the butter has melted completely. Add the spinach and cook for 3 minutes, or until it has wilted. Mix in the horseradish and cook for 3 minutes more, combining thoroughly.

5 ➜ Slice the steaks into 1-inch strips. Divide the steak and spinach between two plates and serve.

NOTES

Resting is always the final step when cooking a steak. In addition to giving the steak a much deserved break after a load of hard work, resting increases juiciness, maximizes flavor, and evens out the cooking. As with any meat, the internal temperature will increase slightly after you take it off the heat, so feel free to try taking your steak off the pan just before it reaches the temperature you are aiming for, then checking to make sure it lands where you want it.

Do not make horse sounds while eating the horseradish. It's one of those things that nobody finds funny. Also, don't pretend you're suddenly a horse expert just because you're eating something with the word "horse" in it. Nobody is impressed. Just relax and be yourself. Talk about things that interest you, or better yet, just listen for once in your life. You don't always have to be the center of attention.

What's that quote about the weight that words have when a quiet person speaks? *The less you say, the more out of practice your mouth is and the higher the likelihood that you'll royally screw up whatever you were trying to get across.*

Whoever said that, don't listen to that guy. He was probably a huge blabbermouth, so you can't really trust him anyway.

CALAMARI

Seafood is a marketing term that was invented to convince people that ocean creatures are edible, rather than the stuff nightmares are made of. When humans first started eating sea creatures, all of which look like some form of horror movie alien, they had to overcome their natural instinct to attack them with fire. While this reflex is genetically ingrained it has been largely repressed through years of conditioning. It is also the reason why sea creatures spend their entire lives hiding inside water.

To be clear: Fish are not sea creatures. They are graceful, delicious, water-slicing, self-propelling arrows. Crabs, lobsters, shrimp, squid, and octopuses are sea creatures. Squid and octopuses are a type of sea creature known as cephalopods, and cephalopods are among the smartest creatures on the planet. Leaving cephalopods to live out their lives in the ocean might allow them to develop an advanced underwater culture that could be a future tourist destination for humans, which could give the ocean a real economic boost. Or we might discover that they are, in fact, aliens, who might one day give us access to their space-travel portal. If we eat them all, we'll never know.

SERVES NO ONE

1 (any size) squid

1 (large) body of salt water

1 ➜ Observe squid in a large body of salty water, such as an ocean. Allow it to swim freely for all of its natural life until it dies of old age or gets eaten by a seafaring predator or a really ambitious horse.

2 ➜ Make yourself Avocado Coupe de Dieu (page 84) instead.

SPAGHETTI
WITH BOLOGNISH SAUCE

Bolognish sauce is often confused with Bolognese sauce. Bolognese sauce originated in the eighteenth century near Bologna, Italy, the birthplace of old-fashioned baloney. Bolognish sauce, on the other hand, originated right now. While these sauces contain most of the same ingredients, look similar, taste similar, and one of them was directly inspired by the other, that's where the similarities end.

The most important difference between these two sauces is how they are made. Bolognese sauce is never stirred using a silicone or plastic wangjangler, because the secret to its flavor is soggy wood. When sauce is made with a wooden wangjangler it is not only infused with the taste of wood sog, but it is also infused with microscopic particles of every sauce that wooden wangjangler has ever come into contact with, adding the rich taste of history. Bolognish sauce, by contrast, is traditionally wangjangled with a nonwooden utensil, which results in a taste that is refreshingly present and in the moment.

SERVES 4

2 tablespoons olive oil

2 garlic cloves, chopped

1 medium yellow onion, diced

1 pound lean ground beef

2 cups shredded carrots from 2 medium carrots

1 (28-ounce) can crushed tomatoes

1½ tablespoons oregano

1 tablespoon plus 1 teaspoon fine sea salt

½ cup chopped fresh parsley

½ cup white wine, such as sauvignon blanc

1 teaspoon freshly ground pepper

¼ teaspoon crushed red pepper flakes

1 (1-pound) box spaghetti

1 cup shredded parmesan

1 ➜ Heat olive oil in a large saucepan over medium heat until it shimmers like the flash and dazzle of a Vegas magician. Add the garlic and onions, and sauté for 7 to 10 minutes, stirring occasionally, until the onions are soft and translucent.

2 ➜ Increase the heat to medium-high, add in the beef, breaking it up into small pieces with your wangjangler, and cook for 5 minutes, until completely browned. Add the carrots and combine thoroughly, cooking for 2 minutes until soft. Add the tomatoes, oregano, 1 teaspoon salt, parsley, white wine, pepper, and chili flakes, then wangjangle thoroughly until the sauce starts to bubble, about 3 minutes. Reduce the heat to low and simmer, covered, for 15 minutes, stirring occasionally. Uncover and simmer for about 30 minutes more, stirring occasionally, until the sauce thickens. What's the occasion? The occasion is stirring.

3 ➜ Meanwhile, make the spaghetti. Fill a large saucepan with 14 cups of water, add the remaining 1 tablespoon of salt, and bring to a boil over high heat. Add the spaghetti and let the water return to a boil, then reduce the heat to medium-high and cook for 8 to 10 minutes, until the pasta is al dente. Drain the pasta, and divide the spaghetti between plates.

4 ➜ Spoon the sauce over the spaghetti and add parmesan to taste.

DESSERTS

Don't be fooled by modern cooking shows that show angry chefs barking orders and ruling the kitchen with fear. This never actually happens.

Modern chefs employ a series of tricks (spatula flips, oven-closing twirls, and ostentatious squeezing techniques) to dazzle the other kitchen workers in order to assert dominance in the kitchen and maintain respect.

A new head chef is selected when successfully challenged. A sous-chef, after painstakingly practicing his or her own unique kitchen tricks in secret (often while acting outwardly clumsy while at work) may challenge the head chef in the midst of a busy dinner rush. With the rest of the kitchen staff looking on with one eye while continuing to cook and plate meals with the other, the challenger will step up and initiate a spatula flip-off or another complicated move that surpasses anything the current chef has displayed so far. The chef is forced to defend his or her position, or lose status immediately.

But no chef worth their weight in salt will have revealed their best, most complicated tricks, which is why most challengers are left humiliated, and must continue sous-cheffing for another year until challenge season opens again. There is so much about chef culture we're only beginning to understand. Until more sociologists learn how to dice onions and get themselves into sous-chef positions, there's plenty that will remain a mystery.

What does this story have to do with dessert? Not much.

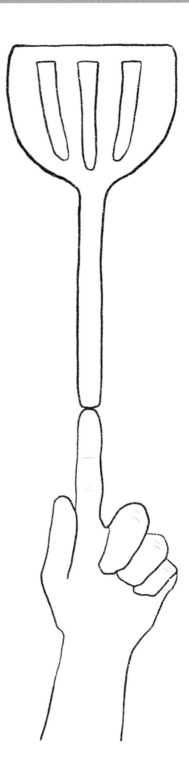

CARAMELIZED PEACHES

WITH VANILLA ICE CREAM

One time when I was hanging out with some friends, we had a whole box of peaches on our hands and an entire bucket of time. We discussed making a dessert and I became very excited. My mom had recently made the most delicious peaches, so I told everyone I would call her to get the amazing recipe. Everyone was thrilled. I called my mom and she told me the recipe. It was sliced peaches with sugar.

I told my friends and they laughed at me. It was then that I realized that not only could you make a really delicious dessert with just a couple ingredients, but also that these were not my real friends. They were simply people using me to get my mom's delicious, and easy, peaches recipe (which I won't share here, on account of it being a family secret).

No matter how many times my so-called friends tried to convince me that they just found it funny, and didn't mean any harm by it, I've stuck to my guns and have been without friends ever since. That's what self-respect looks like.

SERVES 2

1 tablespoon unsalted butter

2 peaches, diced

2 teaspoons brown sugar

2 scoops vanilla ice cream

1 → In a small nonstick skillet, melt the butter over medium heat. Add the peaches and stir to coat. Sprinkle the brown sugar evenly on the peaches, and cook for 5 minutes, or until the peaches start to brown.

2 → Divide the ice cream between two bowls and spoon the hot peaches over the ice cream, then serve. Enjoy the delicious contrast of hot things and cold things getting along for once. Also enjoy the friendship of whoever you're sharing it with who won't make fun of this recipe.

FROZEN COCONUT FUDGE

TYPE STUFF

The dictionary says fudge is made from sugar, butter, milk, or cream. I say the dictionary is living in the past, man. Because that's when fudge was invented. In the past.

Frozen Coconut Fudge Type Stuff is a reasonable facsimile of fudge, but only visually, and from a bit of a distance. It's frozen because if it gets to room temperature and your room isn't cold, it will probably melt. And even when it's frozen, it's melty to the touch, so eat it with a knife and fork if you want to keep your fingers pristine—and also if you want to have your reputation as a chill, laid-back person irreparably trashed.

MAKES 8 PIECES

½ cup coconut oil

½ cup smooth peanut butter, preferably natural

2 tablespoons unsweetened cocoa powder

2 tablespoons maple syrup

½ teaspoon pure vanilla extract

Pinch of fine sea salt

1 ➜ In a small freezer-safe dish, combine the coconut oil, peanut butter, cocoa powder, maple syrup, and vanilla and wangjangle thoroughly. Sprinkle the salt in a fine layer on top.

2 ➜ Freeze for 3 hours, or until the liquid has solidified from the freezing because that's what happens when things get cold.

3 ➜ Cut into squares and eat cold.

NOTES

It's easy to make a sugar-free version by swapping out the maple syrup for stevia drops.

It's easy to make a cocoa-free version by swapping out the cocoa powder for ground muskox.

For a calorie-free version of this recipe see Diet Ice Pops (page 203).

CHOCO-BANANA
ICE CREAM

There's no cream in this stuff. But it does have a creamy texture. But if something has a creamy texture without having cream in it, is the texture actually creamy? Or are we describing something else, such as smoothness?

If I changed the recipe title to Choco-Banana Ice Smoothness, would it still taste as good? That depends on your feelings toward smoothness. Words are known to affect the flavor of food because the brain is the biggest spice rack of all.

SERVES 3

2 bananas, sliced and frozen overnight

1 tablespoon unsweetened cocoa powder

¼ cup almond milk or coconut milk or any kind of milk

¼ teaspoon pure vanilla extract (optional)

1 ➜ In a food processor, combine the bananas, cocoa powder, milk, and vanilla and process until smooth.

2 ➜ Transfer the mixture to a bowl and serve immediately.

NOTES

You are going to want to eat this dessert right away—don't freeze it then eat it. If you do that, then the amazing texture will be ruined by ice crystals.

But don't judge ice crystals just because they could ruin the dessert. They have a very important function in life, mainly that of existing in a crystallized state. This is the only time you see water molecules formed into a quiet, hexagonal pattern, rather than roaming the earth, recklessly flexing their destructive power.

It's not that water molecules intend to be destructive, it's just that there's so many of them. If we could reduce the amount of water molecules on the planet, we could reduce the amount of hurricanes. That's just common sense.

DIET
ICE POPS

Eating a diet ice pop is a great way to enjoy a delicious dessert while watching your figure. You can eat up to four diet ice pops a day without significantly increasing your caloric intake. The transparency of the ice pops allows you to see all of the ingredients, so you know exactly what you're eating. Congratulations, you're eating a diet ice pop.

MAKES 8 ICE POPS

2 cups water

1 → Pour water into an 8-pop ice pop mold. Freeze for 4 hours, until solid.

2 → Run the ice pop mold under warm water for 20 seconds to loosen diet ice pops.

3 → Serve immediately, or at any time if eaten inside a freezer.

MINI
ICE CREAM
SANDWICHES

My kids LOVE these! They'll come inside from shooting hoops on the driveway and be all like "Dad! Dad! Can you make the ice cream sandwiches?" I'm like "No way!" But I don't really mean it. I'm already reaching for the ice cream.

Cody will ask if we can go for a bike ride later. Melissa wants to come, too. Why not? It's a nice day. It's a nice life. It's a great time to ride a bike. Cody rides really fast, cruising up ahead of us. He's got so much energy from those ice cream sandwiches, and they're pretty healthy thanks to the ginger. Melissa and I hang back, talking about how school's going. Cody circles back and pretends he's going to crash into us, then swerves at the last second. "Be careful, Cody!" We like to have fun.

It's around then that I wake up. Sweating. Alone. I reach to my side but no one is there. Just a cold, empty plate. I let out a huge sigh of relief and fall back asleep, wondering how late I'll sleep in.

MAKES 12 SANDWICHES

1½ cups caramel or butterscotch ice cream

24 ginger snaps

1 → Spread about 1 tablespoon ice cream on the bottom of a ginger snap so it's ½ inch thick, then press another ginger snap on top to complete the sandwich. Assemble the rest of the ice cream sandwiches, then place them in a container and freeze for 4 hours, until the cookies soften. But won't the cookies harden in the freezer? No, they won't. That's why I said they will soften. Because I know what I'm talking about.

2 → Serve the sandwiches cold, because they have ice cream in them and that's the temperature of ice cream. Serve the sandwiches at room temperature for Cream Sandwiches.

MUG FULL OF
BLUEBERRY
BROWNIES

Blueberries and brownies follow one of the laziest naming traditions of all time, commonly known as "let's just call it the color that it is." It's sad when you consider that these foods, both of which are necessary for survival, have impressive naming potential. Blueberries could have been sweet bursty bites, rolly drops, or ball berries. Brownies could have been snacky squares, chocolate bread, or depressed cake. But here we are, naming these foods based on their shallow appearance, rather than what's really going on inside.

SERVES 1

3 tablespoons all-purpose flour

3 tablespoons brown sugar of choice

3 tablespoons unsweetened cocoa powder

2 tablespoons unsalted butter, melted

3 tablespoons 2% milk

Pinch of fine sea salt

¼ cup blueberries

1 ➙ In your second-least-favorite mug, combine the flour, brown sugar, cocoa powder, melted butter, milk, and salt. Use a spoon to wangjangle the ingredients until they transform into a thick batter, much like the transformation of the caterpillar into a butterfly, except with fewer wings and less crunch.

2 ➙ Add the blueberries and work them into the batter until they are completely combined. If they smush apart, that's great. If they don't smush apart, that's also great.

3 ➙ Heat the batter in the microwave on high for 1 minute 20 seconds, until all of the batter has turned cakey. If it isn't cooked through, repeat until it is, checking on it every 20 seconds.

4 ➙ Allow the brownie to cool for 10 minutes, then eat it out of the mug with a spoon, or dump it into a miniature loaf pan and pretend you're a baker.

NOTFOGATO

Scrivo questa nota in italiano per compensare, con la raffinatezza della lingua, l'utilizzo del caffè istantaneo. Questo, molto probabilmente, farà rigirare gli italiani nelle tombe. Non quelli che sono vivi. Loro semplicemente si rigireranno per strada, modo tradizionale per preparare il corpo a consumare l'affogato, il dolce fatto con l'espresso e su cui si basa questa ricetta.

Se ti interessa preparare il corpo nel modo tradizionale, non rigirarti troppo. Fallo solo quanto basta per bruciare un po' di calorie e aumentare l'appetito, ma non tanto da farti venire le vertigini. È necessario mantenere un coordinamento sufficiente per utilizzare un cucchiaio.

SERVES 1

1 ounce (2 tablespoons) boiling water

1 teaspoon instant coffee granules

1 scoop vanilla ice cream

0 shame

1 → In a mug or small bowl, combine the boiling water and instant coffee and stir until the coffee is completely dissolved. (If you own an espresso maker, feel free to use a shot of espresso instead. You can also use an ounce or two of drip coffee made at four times the strength.)

2 → Scoop the ice cream into your vessel. Swirl the ice cream around until the coffee gets creamy and thickens, then serve with a spoon.

POLVERE DI CAFFÈ ISTANTANEO

PEANUT BUTTER COCONUT
COOKIES

Free cookies make people flip their lids. If you make a batch of these, then go into your office and walk around offering them to people, their faces will light up as if you are giving out free money. But really, it will just be free cookies.

When people who can't eat dairy or gluten find out that these cookies are safe for them, they will positively frigging lose it since they usually can't eat free cookies. So make sure you don't offer these cookies to anyone who can't eat dairy or gluten, because you don't want to reward people who can't control their emotions.

MAKES 2 DOZEN COOKIES

1 cup smooth peanut butter, preferably natural

½ cup packed brown sugar

½ cup sweetened coconut flakes

1 large egg

½ teaspoon fine sea salt

1 ➡ Preheat the oven to 325°F. Line a baking sheet with parchment paper.

2 ➡ In a medium bowl, combine the peanut butter, brown sugar, coconut, egg, and salt and wangjangle until smooth. Roll the mixture into 1-inch balls between your palms, place on the prepared baking sheet, and press with a fork until ¾ inch thick. If the dough is too sticky, use a teaspoon to shape the balls. If the teaspoon is too sticky, you're screwed.

3 ➡ Bake for 12 to 15 minutes, until the balls start to brown. Remove from the oven and allow them to cool for 10 minutes before serving. Then hoard them. Your cookies, your choice.

CHOCOLATE CHILI GINGER

PRETZELS

As a child I couldn't imagine living a life where I could make chocolate-covered pretzels at literally any time of the day or night. That's because even then, I wisely knew this wasn't possible.

To make chocolate-covered pretzels you must be awake, for starters, which rules out one-third of your time. You probably can't be at work, you shouldn't be driving a car, and you should not make chocolate-covered pretzels when a close friend is telling you about their problems, unless their problem is that they don't have any chocolate-covered pretzels.

You can't make them at a wedding, when you're at the hospital, or while attending a sporting event. But aside from those examples, you can make chocolate-covered pretzels any time of the day or night. These restrictions may sound sad, at first. But chocolate-covered pretzels are very special, so appreciate the restrictions. They keep you from making them so often you become numb to their greatness.

MAKES 1½ CUPS FREAKING AMAZING PRETZELS

4 ounces semisweet baking chocolate

½ teaspoon chili powder

½ teaspoon ground ginger

1 cup mini salted pretzels

Salt to taste (optional)

1 ➤ Line a baking sheet with parchment paper.

2 ➤ In a small saucepan, melt the chocolate over low heat, stirring constantly, for about 7 minutes, or until completely smooth (see notes on page 212). Add the chili powder and ground ginger, then wangjangle until combined thoroughly, about 1 minute more.

3 ➤ Remove the pan from the heat and allow the sauce to cool for 10 minutes, until it thickens slightly, then add ½ cup of the pretzels. Fold them in until they are completely coated in chocolate.

4 ➤ Using a fork, fish out the pretzels and lay them on the baking sheet. It's okay if some are overlapped or stacked, they'll snap apart no problem. Don't stress. Relax. It's just dessert. Don't get all intense about it.

5 ➤ Add the remaining pretzels to the chocolate and repeat. Use a spoon to drizzle any remaining chocolate onto the pretzels, and sprinkle salt on top, if desired.

6 ➤ Place the baking sheet inside the fridge to cool for at least 1 hour, then serve.

(RECIPE CONTINUES)

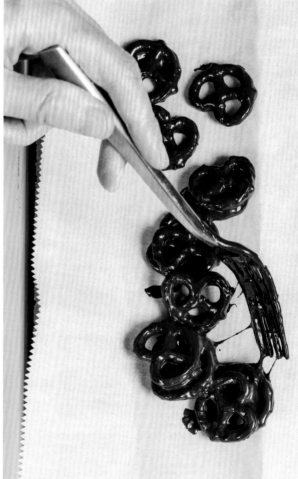

NOTES

When you're melting the chocolate directly in a saucepan, it's best to mentally prepare yourself for what will inevitably happen. Someone who thinks they're smarter than you will wander by and try to tell you that you can create your own "double boiler" by floating a saucepan inside a bigger, water-filled saucepan, and that it's a better way to melt chocolate because it will keep the chocolate from burning because water only heats up to 212°F, which isn't high enough to burn the chocolate.

Restrain yourself. Quietly, but firmly, point out that melting the chocolate on low heat is simpler and easier, that you don't run the risk of getting any water in the chocolate, which can ruin the batch even in small quantities, and that it's one less pot to deal with afterward.

Then throw the pot of chocolate with all of your strength against the opposite kitchen wall. This should send a firm but clear message that you know what you're doing, and nothing is going to stop you from making it the way you know works best.

Not even good advice.

CHOCOLATE CAKEY LOAF
TYPE THING

If you are the kind of person who bakes a lot of cakes (which you are not, because if you were, you'd be reading a different book), then you might be thinking I accidentally left the eggs out of this recipe. The truth is I left them out on purpose, even though my friend Julia said "you need eggs," when I told her I was trying to figure out how to make this cake a bit fluffier.

And while there aren't eggs in this cake, I highly recommend sprinkling broken egg shells all around the perimeter of the cake when you serve it, so that people won't think it's a sub-par cake due to their egg-related brainwashing. Also, doing so lets everybody know that all of the eggshells are on the outside of the cake, rather than inside of the cake.

MAKES 1 (9-INCH) CHOCOLATE CAKEY LOAF TYPE THING

1½ **cups all-purpose flour**

1¼ **cups white sugar**

¾ **cup unsweetened cacao powder**

1 **teaspoon baking soda**

1 **teaspoon fine sea salt**

1 **cup chopped walnuts**

½ **cup dark chocolate chips or chunks**

1½ **cups unsweetened vanilla almond milk**

½ **cup vegetable oil**

1 **teaspoon pure vanilla extract**

1 **teaspoon white or apple cider vinegar**

¼ **cup raspberry jam**

1 ➜ Preheat the oven to 350°F. Coat a 9-inch loaf pan with cooking spray.

2 ➜ In a large bowl, stir together the flour, sugar, cacao powder, baking soda, salt, walnuts, and chocolate chips. Use a fork to sift until well combined. Sifting means lifting from the bottom while mixing to get a bunch of air into the ingredients as you mix, as opposed to attempting to find gold, which is what you do when you make Yukon Pie.

3 ➜ In a medium bowl, combine the almond milk, oil, vanilla extract, vinegar, and jam, then whisk passionately until the oil has been incorporated.

4 ➜ Create a divot in the center of the dry ingredients and pour the wet ingredients in the divot. Using a spatula, fold the ingredients together until just mixed, being careful not to overmix. It's okay if there's still some bits of dry ingredients if it's mostly evenly combined. Avoid wangjangling. This is the first and last time you will ever see those two words together.

5 ➜ Pour the batter into the prepared pan and bake for 65 to 75 minutes, until a toothpick jabbed into the center comes out clean.

6 ➜ When the cake is finished, allow it to cool for 20 minutes before sliding it out of the loaf pan onto literally any surface that's not too dirty, and allow it to cool for an hour before serving.

NOTES

Much like the fork with potatoes, the toothpick is the Ultimate Determiner of Doneness. If you cook this cakey loaf for an hour and a half, and your toothpick is still coming out covered in batter, it's not done. Also your oven is broken. Also make sure you use a clean toothpick each time you test it. Also resist the temptation to test it before the cake has completely risen. Also don't open your oven door more often than necessary because every time you do the temperature drops, which increases your cooking time.

When the cake is finished, it will probably have a crevice across the top. This doesn't mean the cake is broken. It means that the cake has finally arrived at its most expansive state. That's the scar of a cake that's lived some life.

Take a quiet moment to remember how soft and vulnerable it was when it was merely batter, and appreciate how strong and full it is in its current form. Sifted from dirt. Combined into goo. Forged in an oven. Baked to perfection.

Does it remind you of anything? Because it reminds me of something. It reminds me of you.

It reminds me of the state you were in when you first picked up this book. You were soft, vulnerable, covered in cake batter. And at some point, you took a shower. You changed your clothes. You learned a thing or two, or didn't learn anything and simply judged. Either way, you're a little more grown up now. A little stronger. A little smarter. A lot cleaner. You're just like a full-grown cake.

Or at least, I really hope.

ACKNOWLEDGMENTS

It takes a village to write a book. Or make a baby. Or raze a barn. It's more than just writing words until you've fulfilled your contractual obligations. It's about a community, and that's why I want to acknowledge you.

You may have sent me recipe ideas and cooking tips or helplessly watched as I stole one from you. Perhaps you edited my book proposal, my first draft, or translated English into Italian while being stone-cold Italian. Perhaps you gave me a cabin to write in where I was scared of being murdered or a house to stay in while I accidentally underfed your dog. Or maybe you invited me to your mountain matador library.

You may have made me a cutting board, sent me an engraved wangjangler, gave me feedback, offered ideas, advice, and encouragement, leant me your dog, leant me your kitchen, asked me to cook yams, collaborated with me in your garage, built me a furnace space ship, shot me with a laser beam, or said, "This needs some acid," while blending herb dressing in a cabin that time in July.

You might have reminded me to eat or made me a meal while I appeared to be writing but was actually wasting time online. Or maybe you gamified texting to help me focus through distraction. Or perhaps you made me food since birth or rightfully told me to tone down my salty language, in addition to countless helpful and supportive things throughout the years. Or maybe you're on my ghostwriting team and that's why this book is haunted.

To all of you—family, friends, loved ones, ghosts—thank you so much.

At Clarkson Potter I'd like to thank Amanda Englander for championing this project, along with Gabrielle Van Tassel, Stephanie Huntwork, Francesca Truman, Mark McCauslin, Kelli Tokos, Erica Gelbard, Daniel Wikey, and Eleanor Thacher for all of your work, patience, editing, designing, ideas, and everything that goes into making a book.

Thanks the photography team of Andy Lee, Thom Driver, Angie Mosier, and Dave Crawford for the great photos, propping, styling, rides, and laughs. Thanks to Allison Renzulli for taste-testing skills.

Thanks to Anthony Mattero for the adept agenting, along with Alex Rice. And Randi Siegel for the impossibly thorough and dedicated managerial prowess.

And to everyone who's been watching, I appreciate it enormously and constantly. And to those of you who are reading this book, I am especially proud of you. For reading. For some reason that's supposed to be a good thing to do.

I'd also like to thank the lumberjacks. Without their constant jacking of lumber, we wouldn't have books. And what kind of world would we live in without books? A sad, sad world with a lot more trees.

And finally I'd like to thank the early humans, now long passed, who first discovered food and decided to try eating it. Without them, this book would never have been possible.

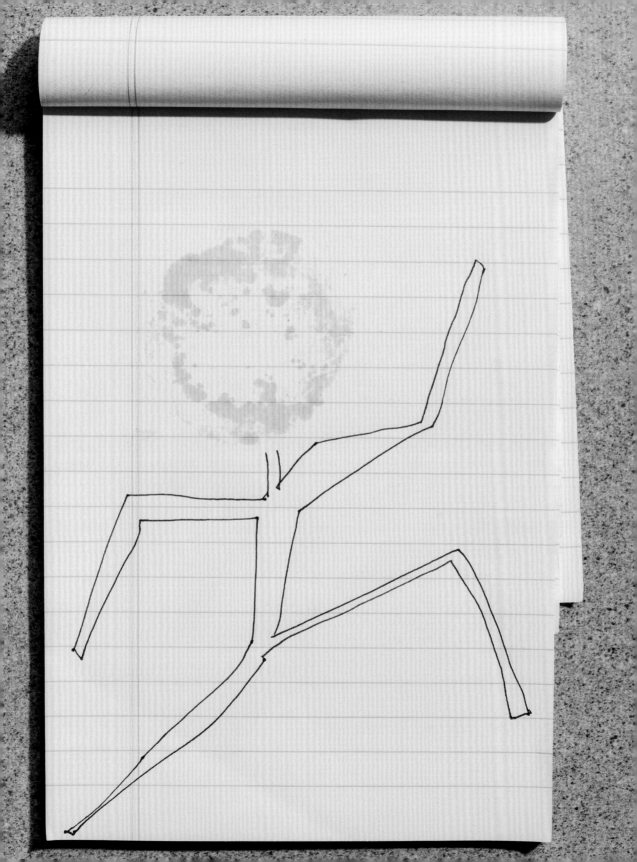

INDEX

A

Acid, and flavor, **34**
Almonds
    Chia "Cereal" "Pudding" "Oatmeal" Type Deal, **69**
    Sliced, Roasted Asparagus with, **140**
Asparagus, Roasted, with Sliced Almonds, **140**
ASSS system of food flavor, **34**
Avocado(s)
    Breakfast Sandwich Mediumest, **102**
    Coupe de Dieu, **84**
    Third Easiest Salad Dressing on Earth, **121**
    Turkey Romaine Slab, **105**
    Veggie Rice Bowl, **166**

B

Bacon
    Breakfast Sandwich Mediumest, **102**
    Leeky Pocket, **108–9**
Baking sheet, **25**
Banana(s)
    Blueberry Smoothie, **56**
    Choco-, Ice Cream, **201**
Basil, in Pesto, **53**
Bean(s). See also Chickpea(s)
    Beanshuka Marinara, **67–68**
    Black, and Rice, Panic-Fried, **162**
    Dip, The, Formerly Known as Gregg's, **76**
    Loaded Cauliflower Bake, **163–64**
    String, Roasted Mustard, **142**
Beef
    Meat and Potatoes, **184**
    Pan-Seared Strip Loin with Horseradical
        Spinach, **188**
    Spaghetti with Bolognish Sauce, **191**
Blueberry
    Brownies, Mug Full of, **206**
    Smoothie, **56**
Breakfast
    Beanshuka Marinara, **67–68**
    Blueberry Smoothie, **56**
    Breakfast Sandwich Mediumest, **102**
    Broccoli Cheddar Quiche Cupcake Muffin-Type
        Things, **60**
    Chia "Cereal" "Pudding" "Oatmeal" Type Deal, **69**
    Green Eggs, **52**
    Green Smoothie, **57**
    Ham and Cheese Muglet™, **63**
    Potato and Egg Hash, **64**
Broccoli
    Cheddar Quiche Cupcake Muffin-Type Things, **60**
    Cheddar Soup, **128**
    Raw, Salad, Creamy, **125**
    Sesame-Roasted, **148**
    Simple Stir-Fry, **157**
    Spicy Peanut Butter Soup, **135**
Broth, **33**
Brownies, Blueberry, Mug Full of, **206**
Brussamic Sprouts, **143**

C

Cakey Loaf Type Thing, Chocolate, **214**
Calamari, **190**
Carrots
    Simple Stir-Fry, **157**
    Spaghetti with Bolognish Sauce, **191**
    Spicy Peanut Butter Soup, **135**
    Veggie Rice Bowl, **166**
Cauliflower
    Bake, Loaded, **163–64**
    Soup, Lizzy's, **128A–29A**
    Stuffed Peppers, **158**
    Walnut Stuff, Toasted, **150**
Charcuterie Plate, Gas Station, **88**
Cheese. See also Cream cheese
    Beanshuka Marinara, **67–68**
    Breakfast Sandwich Mediumest, **102**
    Broccoli Cheddar Quiche Cupcake Muffin-Type
        Things, **60**
    Broccoli Cheddar Soup, **128**
    Dip, Nobody's, **81**
    Gas Station Charcuterie Plate, **88**

Cheese *(cont.)*
  and Ham Melt, **112**
  and Ham Muglet™, **63**
  Loaded Cauliflower Bake, **163–64**
  Stuffed Peppers, **158**
  Sweet Tomato Pita, Grilled, **115**
Cherries, in Tuna Salad Sandwich, **107**
Chia "Cereal" "Pudding" "Oatmeal" Type Deal, **69**
Chicken
  Breast, Jalepeño, **187**
  Breast, Simple Seared, **174–75**
  cooking times, **172–73**
  Leeky Olive, **183**
  Thighs, Curry, **185**
Chickpea(s)
  and Olive Spread, Ava's Post-Apocalyptic, **80**
  Quinoa Salad, **127**
  and Sausage Curry, **180**
  Spicy Peanut Butter Soup, **135**
Chili Chocolate Ginger Pretzels, **210**
Chocolate
  Cakey Loaf Type Thing, **214**
  Chili Ginger Pretzels, **210**
  Choco-Banana Ice Cream, **201**
  Frozen Coconut Fudge Type Stuff, **200**
  Mug Full of Blueberry Brownies, **206**
Claw grip for knives, **20–21**
Coconut
  Chia "Cereal" "Pudding" "Oatmeal" Type Deal, **69**
  Fudge Type Stuff, Frozen, **200**
  Peanut Butter Cookies, **209**
Coffee, in Notfogato, **207**
Cookies, Peanut Butter Coconut, **209**
Cooking oil, **30**
Cream cheese
  Creampesio Cucumberetta, **87**
  Eddie's Roasted Red Pepper Dip, **77**
  Nobody's Cheese Dip, **81**
Cucumbers. See also Pickles
  Basic Boring Mixed Green Salad, **124**
  Creampesio Cucumberetta, **87**
  Veggie Rice Bowl, **166**
Curry, Sausage and Chickpea, **180**
Curry Chicken Thighs, **185**
Curry Egg Salad Sandwich, **106**
Cutting boards, **26**

D

Desserts
  Caramelized Peaches with Vanilla Ice Cream, **198**
  Choco-Banana Ice Cream, **201**
  Chocolate Cakey Loaf Type Thing, **214**
  Chocolate Chili Ginger Pretzels, **210**
  Diet Ice Pops, **203**
  Frozen Coconut Fudge Type Stuff, **200**
  Mini Ice Cream Sandwiches, **204**
  Mug Full of Blueberry Brownies, **206**
  Notfogato, **207**
  Peanut Butter Coconut Cookies, **209**
Diet Ice Pops, **203**
Dill, Baked Tilapia with, **178**
Dipping Sauce, Sweet Potato Wedges with, **82**
Dips
  The Bean, Formerly Known as Gregg's, **76**
  Cheese, Nobody's, **81**
  Roasted Red Pepper, Eddie's, **77**
Drinks. *See* Smoothies

E

Egg(s)
  Beanshuka Marinara, **67–68**
  Breakfast Sandwich Mediumest, **102**
  Broccoli Cheddar Quiche Cupcake Muffin-Type
    Things, **60**
  Green, **52**
  Ham and Cheese Muglet™, **63**
  and Potato Hash, **64**
  Salad, Curry, Sandwich, **106**

F

Fats, **38**
Fish
  Baked Tilapia with Dill, **178**
  cooking times, **172–73**
  Maple-Baked Salmon, **177**
  Tuna Salad Sandwich, **107**
Frozen Coconut Fudge Type Stuff, **200**

G

Garlic, **32–33**
Gas Station Charcuterie Plate, **88**

Ginger Chocolate Chili Pretzels, **210**
Green Eggs, **52**
Greens
 Basic Boring Mixed Green Salad, **124**
 Green Smoothie, **57**
 Pan-Fried Kale, **147**
 Pan-Seared Strip Loin with Horseradical
  Spinach, **188**
 Turkey Romaine Slab, **105**
Grilled Cheese Sweet Tomato Pita, **115**

H

Ham
 and Cheese Melt, **112**
 and Cheese Muglet™, **63**
Hash, Potato and Egg, **64**
Hot sauce, **33**

I

Ice Cream
 Choco-Banana, **201**
 Notfogato, **207**
 Sandwiches, Mini, **204**
 Vanilla, Caramelized Peaches with, **198**
Ice Pops, Diet, **203**
Instant-read thermometer, **27**

K

Kale, Pan-Fried, **147**
Knives, **17–21**

L

Leek(s)
 cleaning, **110**
 Leeky Bacon Pocket, **108–9**
 Leeky Olive Chicken, **183**

M

Maillard reaction, **39**
Main dishes
 Baked Tilapia with Dill, **178**
 Calamari, **190**
 Curry Chicken Thighs, **185**
 Jalepeño Chicken Breast, **187**
 Leeky Olive Chicken, **183**
 Loaded Cauliflower Bake, **163–64**
 Maple-Baked Salmon, **177**
 Meat and Potatoes, **184**
 Nearly Sauceless Pasta, **160**
 Panic-Fried Black Beans and Rice, **162**
 Pan-Seared Strip Loin with Horseradical
  Spinach, **188**
 Sausage and Chickpea Curry, **180**
 Simple Seared Chicken Breast, **174–75**
 Simple Stir-Fry, **157**
 Spaghetti with Bolognish Sauce, **191**
 Stuffed Peppers, **158**
 Veggie Rice Bowl, **166**
 Zucchini Butter Noodles, **159**
Maple-Baked Salmon, **177**
Marinara Sauce, **68**
Measuring cups and spoons, **27**
Meat. *See also* Bacon; Beef; Ham; Sausage(s)
 cooking times, **172–73**
Mental game of cooking, **40–43**
Microwave, **16**
Mixing bowls, **26**
Mug Full of Blueberry Brownies, **206**
Muglet™, Ham and Cheese, **63**
Mustard String Beans, Roasted, **142**

N

Notfogato, **207**
Nuts
 Chia "Cereal" "Pudding" "Oatmeal" Type Deal, **69**
 Chocolate Cakey Loaf Type Thing, **214**
 Gas Station Charcuterie Plate, **88**
 Roasted Asparagus with Sliced Almonds, **140**
 Toasted Walnut Cauliflower Stuff, **150**

O

Olive(s)
 and Chickpea Spread, Ava's Post-Apocalyptic, **80**
 Leeky Chicken, **183**
 Nearly Sauceless Pasta, **160**
 Quinoa Salad, **127**
Onions, **30–31**
Oven, **16**
Oven gloves, **22**

P

Pan-frying, **46**
Parchment paper, **25**
Pasta
    Nearly Sauceless, **160**
    Spaghetti with Bolognish Sauce, **191**
Peaches, Caramelized, with Vanilla Ice Cream, **198**
Peanut Butter
    Coconut Cookies, **209**
    Frozen Coconut Fudge Type Stuff, **200**
    Soup, Spicy, **135**
Pears
    Green Smoothie, **57**
Pepper, freshly ground, **29–30**
Pepper(s)
    Jalapeño Chicken Breast, **187**
    Loaded Cauliflower Bake, **163–64**
    Nearly Sauceless Pasta, **160**
    Nobody's Cheese Dip, **81**
    Roasted Red, Dip, Eddie's, **77**
    Sausage and Chickpea Curry, **180**
    Simple Stir-Fry, **157**
    Stuffed, **158**
    Veggie Rice Bowl, **166**
Pesto, **53**
Pickles
    adding to sandwiches, **100–101**
    Breakfast Sandwich Mediumest, **102**
    Curry Egg Salad Sandwich, **106**
    Ham and Cheese Melt, **112**
    Potato Salad for the Living, **132**
    Tuna Salad Sandwich, **107**
Pork. See Bacon; Ham; Sausage(s)
Potato(es)
    and Egg Hash, **64**
    Meat and, **184**
    Rosemary Roasted, **149**
    Salad for the Living, **132**
    Sweet, Wedges with Dipping Sauce, **82**
Pretzels, Chocolate Chili Ginger, **210**

Q

Quiche, Broccoli Cheddar, Cupcake Muffin-Type Things, **60**
Quinoa Salad, **127**

R

Rice
    and Black Beans, Panic-Fried, **162**
    Bowl, Veggie, **166**
Roasting, **46**
Romaine Turkey Slab, **105**
Rosemary Roasted Potatoes, **149**
Rubber gloves, **43**

S

Salad Dressings
    Easiest, on Earth, **119**
    Second Easiest, on Earth, **120**
    Third Easiest, on Earth, **121**
Salads
    Mixed Green, Basic Boring, **124**
    Potato, for the Living, **132**
    Quinoa, **127**
    Raw Broccoli, Creamy, **125**
Salmon, Maple-Baked, **177**
Salt
    seasoning with, **29, 35–36**
    types of, **28–29**
Sandwiches
    adding pickles to, **100–101**
    Breakfast, Mediumest, **102**
    Curry Egg Salad, **106**
    fresh, moist bread for, **96**
    Ham and Cheese Melt, **112**
    Leeky Bacon Pocket, **108–9**
    Mini Ice Cream, **204**
    preparing, principles of, **95–101**
    sauces or condiments for, **96**
    spreading condiments on, **98**
    structural integrity, **96–97**
    Sweet Tomato Grilled Cheese Pita, **115**
    Tuna Salad, **107**
    Turkey Romaine Slab, **105**
    types of, **93–94**
Saucepan, **24**
Sauces
    Dipping, Sweet Potato Wedges with, **82**
    Marinara, **68**
    Pesto, **53**
Sausage(s)
    and Chickpea Curry, **180**

Potato Salad for the Living, **132**
Scrub brush, **43**
Seasoning foods, **37–38**
Sesame-Roasted Broccoli, **148**
Sides. *See also* Salads
    Brussamic Sprouts, **143**
    Pan-Fried Kale, **147**
    Roasted Asparagus with Sliced Almonds, **140**
    Roasted Mustard String Beans, **142**
    Rosemary Roasted Potatoes, **149**
    Sesame-Roasted Broccoli, **148**
    Toasted Walnut Cauliflower Stuff, **150**
Skillets, **24**
Smoothies
    Blueberry, **56**
    Green, **57**
Snacks
    Ava's Post-Apocalyptic Chickpea and Olive
        Spread, **80**
    Avocado Coupe de Dieu, **84**
    The Bean Dip Formerly Known as Gregg's, **76**
    Creampesio Cucumberetta, **87**
    Eddie's Roasted Red Pepper Dip, **77**
    Gas Station Charcuterie Plate, **88**
    Nobody's Cheese Dip, **81**
    Sweet Potato Wedges with Dipping Sauce, **82**
Soups
    Broccoli Cheddar, **128**
    Cauliflower, Lizzy's, **128A–29A**
    Peanut Butter, Spicy, **135**
Spatula, **22**
Spinach
    Green Smoothie, **57**
    Horseradical, Pan-Seared Strip Loin with, **188**
Spread, Ava's Post-Apocalyptic Chickpea and Olive, **80**
Stir-Fry, Simple, **157**
Stoves, **15–16**
Stuffed Peppers, **158**
Sweetness, and flavor, **36**
Sweet Potato Wedges with Dipping Sauce, **82**

T

Tasting food, **14**
Thermometer, instant-read, **27**
Tilapia, Baked, with Dill, **178**
Tomato(es)
    Basic Boring Mixed Green Salad, **124**

Breakfast Sandwich Mediumest, **102**
Creampesio Cucumberetta, **87**
Jalepeño Chicken Breast, **187**
Marinara Sauce, **68**
Nearly Sauceless Pasta, **160**
Spaghetti with Bolognish Sauce, **191**
Spicy Peanut Butter Soup, **135**
Sweet, Grilled Cheese Pita, **115**
Tools, **43**
Tuna Salad Sandwich, **107**
Turkey Romaine Slab, **105**

V

Vanilla Ice Cream, Caramelized Peaches with, **198**
Vegetables. *See also* Sides; *specific vegetables*
    Veggie Rice Bowl, **166**

W

Walnut(s)
    Cauliflower Stuff, Toasted, **150**
    Chocolate Cakey Loaf Type Thing, **214**
Wangjangler (spatula), **22**

Z

Zucchini Butter Noodles, **159**